CLYDEBANK
BATTLECRUISERS

CLYDEBANK
BATTLECRUISERS
Forgotten Photographs from
John Brown's Shipyard

Ian Johnston

Naval Institute Press

Frontispiece: *Inflexible* at speed on her
trial runs. (NRS UCS1–118–374–44)

Text © Ian Johnston 2011
Photographs Crown Copyright © 2011 by permission of National Records of Scotland

First published in Great Britain in 2011 by
Seaforth Publishing
An imprint of Pen & Sword Books Ltd
47 Church Street, Barnsley
S Yorkshire S70 2AS

www.seaforthpublishing.com
Email info@seaforthpublishing.com

Published and distributed in the United States of America and Canada
by the Naval Institute Press, 291 Wood Road, Annapolis, Maryland 21402-5034
www.nip.org

LOC number 2011932519

ISBN 978-1-59114-120-4

Typeset and designed by Stephen Dent
Printed in China through Printworks International Ltd

CONTENTS

INTRODUCTION

Below: The river frontage of John Brown's Clydebank shipyard in 1907. The Cunard liner *Lusitania* is in the fitting-out basin which separates the works into West and East Yards. While there are no vessels under construction in the West Yard, the East Yard is well occupied. The shipbuilding berths are served by light pole derricks capable of lifting three tons. The stern of *Inflexible* can be seen to right of shot. See yard plan overleaf. (Author's collection)

During the period 1906 to 1916, five main classes of battlecruisers were built for the Royal Navy, a total of thirteen ships. The orders for these vessels were distributed across the principal shipyards, Royal Dockyards and private yards responsible for all the capital ships built up to and including the First World War. For many of these yards, this meant an all but continuous supply of prestigious contracts, particularly so in the case of battlecruisers which were generally of a higher order value than their battleship equivalents and moreover, held in very high esteem by the Navy and public alike in the years up to 1914.

The very rapid development of the battlecruiser type during the ten-year period from 1906 to 1916 resulted in ships half as long again on twice the displacement, 20 per cent faster and with 50 per cent more offensive power. Naturally, the increase in size that inevitably accompanied successive classes of capital ship had an impact on the yards that produced them to the extent that, by 1916, only a handful of the yards that started building the early dreadnoughts were capable of building ships the size of *Repulse* and *Hood*.

The John Brown shipyard and marine engineering works on the River Clyde is significant in the construction of battlecruisers for two reasons. The first is that the records of this company have survived the collapse of the British shipbuilding industry substantially intact although with some important areas missing. In this, John Brown's is probably better served historically than any of the other big British yards operating at that time. These records provide access to information about the construction of the ships they built in the form of a detailed breakdown of costs and the labour devoted to each contract. The latter, expressed in weekly levels, gives an indication of effort over the entire building period. However, the skills and techniques employed at Clydebank were much the same as those in any of the big British yards and to that extent, the experience of Clydebank can be seen as typical of the rest of the industry as a whole. Secondly, John Brown's is noteworthy in having built one battlecruiser from each of the five main classes beginning with *Inflexible* followed by *Australia*, *Tiger*, *Repulse* and *Hood*. Had the construction of the 'G3' battlecruiser design of 1921 gone ahead, Brown's would also have contributed one of those.

While there are many expert books on the design history and operational careers of battlecruisers, the purpose of this book is to look exclu-

sively at the construction of the five that were laid down over a ten-year period at Clydebank. The working practices, machines and tools used there were typical of those used throughout the shipbuilding industry and to that extent, the events described here could as easily have taken place at any of the other large British yards. While the shipyard was the point of assembly, the ramifications of building such large and complex vessels ran through much of British industry, with companies located throughout the UK making contributions to the ship as disparate as barbette armour and the ship's bell.

The sequence of events from conception of the design of a warship, through the tendering process to the construction, completion and trials is largely the same for all the vessels described here. The information used to describe this process is based on two sources: the Ships' Covers held at the National Maritime Museum in Greenwich and the archives of John Brown & Co Ltd, Clydebank, held at Glasgow University Archives. The Ships' Covers were used to retain documents relevant to individual ships from the conceptual phase through construction and subsequent service careers. They reflect Admiralty thinking through internal memos, letters, reports and other material across a range of subjects pertinent to a particular ship or class of ships. The shipbuilder's records are concerned exclusively with the tendering and construction phases of the ship. Together, both sources throw some light on the relationship between the Admiralty and the shipbuilding firms in what has generally been a neglected area of study. The Covers are, however, somewhat haphazard in their organisation with some documents out of chronological order and others undated. Where the Cover for one ship might give a full report on steam trials, for example, this might be missing entirely in another. The John Brown archive, although voluminous, is also incomplete and inconsistent in part. For those reasons, an even treatment of the five ships that concern this

book is not possible. However, a particular strength of the John Brown Archive is the large number of glass plate negatives which record the building process from keel laying to trials. These excellent images provide the pictorial basis for this book.

John Brown & Co Ltd

By the time *Inflexible* was laid down at their Clydebank shipyard in 1906, the yard had been in existence since 1871. Many prestigious liners had been constructed over the years and a lasting relationship had been formed with Cunard, the most recent example of which was the order for *Lusitania*. However, the Clydebank works did not assume the title John Brown & Co Ltd until 1899 when the Sheffield company of that name purchased the yard for a little under £1 million. The Sheffield company wanted a secure outlet for their steel forge and armour products and correctly foresaw a great opportunity in warship construction not simply because of the Royal Navy's pre-eminent position in the fleets of the world but also in the emerging naval race between Britain and Germany. During the 1890s a number of well-known British companies with armour and armament manufacturing capacities had also ventured into shipbuilding, such as Vickers at Barrow and Cammell at Birkenhead, as a means of extending and consolidating output. In all probability, the reality of this contest as measured by the volume of warship orders that ensued exceeded their wildest dreams.

Even before the acquisition of Clydebank by John Brown, the yard had completed an interesting number of warship orders. From the mid-1880s, onwards, a series of small cruisers were built for the Admiralty as well as a protected cruiser for the Spanish (*Reina Regente*) and Japanese (*Chiyoda*) navies. More orders followed for larger vessels including *Terrible* (1897) and many torpedo-boat destroyers. The first battleship

order was *Ramillies* (1892), followed by *Jupiter* (1895), *Asahi* (1899) for the Japanese government and *Hindustan* (1903). Under the ownership of John Brown & Co Ltd, the Clydebank Works had a high degree of autonomy although major decision making was referred to the main John Brown Board, under the chairmanship of Lord Aberconway, which met at either the Sheffield Works or at the company's London offices at The Sanctuary.

By 1906, the Clydebank Works covered 80 acres comprising two yards separated by a fitting-out basin and a large engine and boiler works. The town of Clydebank grew up around the shipyard which by 1899 had a population of 19,000. By 1906, the Clydebank Works was well equipped, highly efficient and an experienced shipbuilding and marine engineering facility employing up to 10,000 workers.

Sir Thomas Bell

The Managing Director of the John Brown works at Clydebank was Thomas Bell, knighted in 1918 for his services to the nation as Deputy Controller of Dockyards and War Shipbuilding for the period 1917–19.

Bell was a marine engineer and responsible for the introduction of the Brown Curtis turbine to Clydebank. This turbine found favour with the Admiralty and was used in propelling *Tiger*, *Repulse* and *Hood* as well as many other warships. Bell attributed the success of his firm in winning these orders to that turbine. In 1919, on his return as Managing Director of the Clydebank works, he said that 'Clydebank stood in the Admiralty records easy first, not alone for excellence of work but what was at that time of still greater importance, absolute fidelity to their promises of dates of delivery.'

The Naval Construction Industry

Britain's pre-eminent position in the fleets of the world, both naval and mercantile, ensured a very large shipbuilding industry. While the Royal Dockyards had traditionally built the ships the Royal Navy required, increasingly the private shipyards were participating in warship building programmes. The Admiralty nurtured these firms by ensuring sufficient orders were distributed across the industry. To be eligible to build warships, a builder had to be on the Admiralty List. This required that a

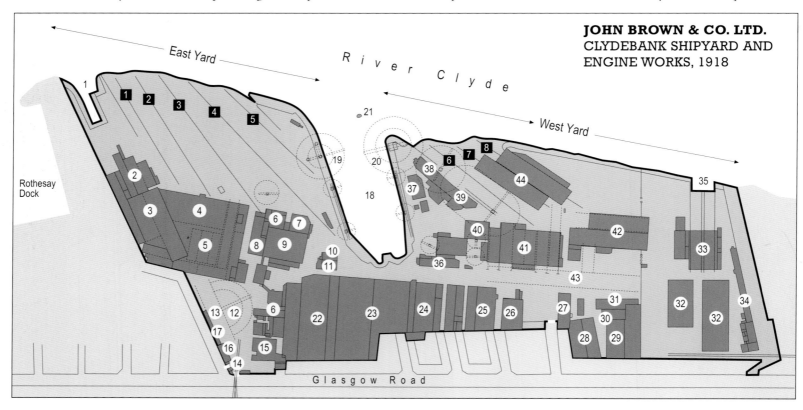

JOHN BROWN & CO. LTD.
CLYDEBANK SHIPYARD AND
ENGINE WORKS, 1918

1. Timber Basin	12. Plate Racks	23. Engine Shops	34. Experimental Tank
2. General Smithy	13. Gantry	24. Foundry	35. Timber Basin
3. Platers Sheds	14. Main Entrance	25. Sheet Iron Shop	36. Rigger's loft
4. East Machine Shed	15. Engine Works Pattern Shop	26. Dressing Shop	37. Dock Workshop
5. Furnaces and Scrieve Boards	16. Electrical Drawing Office	27. Brass Finishing Shop	38. Plumbers Shop
6. Offices	17. Admiralty Overseers Offices	28. Stores	39. Shipwrights' Shop
7. General Store	18. Fitting-out Basin	29. Funnel Shed	40. Beam Shed
8. Shipyard Engineers	19. 150-ton Derrick Crane	30. Shafting Shop	41. West Machine Shop
9. Joiners Shop	20. 150-ton Cantilever Crane	31. Condenser Shop	42. Platers Shed
10. Dock Engineers	21. Mole	32. Timber Drying Sheds	43. Plate Gantry
11. Engine Works Store	22. Boiler Shops	33. Saw Mill	44. Covered Berths

■1 Building berths

(Drawing by the author)

Above: A midships view taken on 13 July 1916 of *Repulse* with two 'R' class destroyers fitting out alongside. Painting is underway on the forward superstructure including bridge, tripod foremast and fore funnel. The spotting top of the monitor *Erebus*, brought to Clydebank to have her 15in mounting fitted can be seen bottom left. (NRS UCS1-118-443-275)

Above: In this 1918 view from the stern of a river steamer, the 150-ton cantilever fitting-out crane dominates the skyline with the East Yard behind. Reflecting the heavier loads being lifted, the shipbuilding berths have now been equipped with steel lattice derricks capable of lifting five tons. (Imperial War Museum Q19400)

shipbuilder had the requisite experience and suitable plant and facilities for any given class of warship or equivalent experience in mercantile work. Constructing the battle fleet that went to sea in the First World War, required the resources of a large portion of the private shipbuilding industry in addition to the Royal Dockyards. The following firms in addition to Portsmouth and Devonport Dockyards, participated in the construction of battlecruisers and battleships from 1906 onwards.

Armstrong Whitworth, Elswick and Walker (no associated engine or
    boiler works)
Beardmore, Dalmuir
John Brown, Clydebank
Cammell Laird, Birkenhead
Fairfield, Govan
Palmers, Jarrow
Scotts, Greenock
Thames Iron Works, Blackwall
Vickers Son & Maxim, Barrow in Furness

Other major shipbuilders such as Harland & Wolff and Swan Hunter & Wigham Richardson, who were on the Admiralty List, either declined to tender or were unsuccessful in winning contracts.

While the shipyards brought ships into existence, vital parts of the ship such as armour and armament were manufactured elsewhere and transported by rail or sea to the shipyard concerned. There were five large armour-rolling mills in Britain at the time of the First World War but only three firms capable of manufacturing heavy gun mountings. The same applied to the construction of main propelling machinery. While most of the large shipbuilding firms mentioned here had inte-

grated or associated engine and boiler works, some did not. Where a warship contract was awarded to a shipbuilder without an engine works, it was the shipyard's responsibility to sub-contract this work to an engine works acceptable to the Admiralty. The Royal Dockyards relied on private firms for the manufacture of engines and boilers and, for example, when the contract to build the battlecruiser *Indefatigable* was given to Devonport Dockyard, the machinery contract was won by John Brown at Clydebank.

The Coventry Ordnance Works (Coventry Syndicate)

Armstrong Whitworth and Vickers Son & Maxim effectively cornered the market for the design and manufacture of heavy gun mountings, highly complex and time-consuming mechanisms to construct. This conferred a distinct advantage to these firms when tendering for warship contracts. In an attempt to break this monopoly, John Brown, Cammell Laird and Fairfield developed the Coventry Ordnance Works from 1905 with the capacity to design and construct guns and mountings. The Works comprised an ordnance factory at Coventry where mountings were designed and guns manufactured. A new ordnance works was built at Scotstoun, on the Clyde where mountings were assembled and tested in gun pits from where they would be taken by barge or ship to the shipyards.

Hundreds of other firms were involved in the supply or manufacture of materials and products for HM ships. Together, the industry that produced warships in Britain was a very large one that in the years before and during the First World War accounted for a significant portion of the public purse. The decade and a half prior to 1914 was dominated by intense naval rivalry between Britain and Germany, which had begun in 1897 when the German legislature passed the first of Admiral Tirpitz's Naval Laws. These, in effect, committed Germany to building a fleet to rival the British. While this initially seemed an impossible target to meet, the British battlefleet was made obsolete by the British themselves with the introduction of the all-big-gun battleship *Dreadnought* in 1906. This

PRINCIPAL ARMOUR AND ARMAMENT COMPANIES:

Armstrong

Ordnance:	Elswick Works, Newcastle
Armour and Forgings:	Openshaw Works, Manchester
Gun Mountings:	Elswick Works, Newcastle

Vickers

Ordnance:	River Don Works, Sheffield
Armour and Forgings:	River Don Works, Sheffield
Gun Mountings:	Barrow

Beardmore

Ordnance:	Parkhead Works, Glasgow
Armour and Forgings:	Parkhead Works, Glasgow

John Brown

Armour and Forgings:	Atlas Works, Sheffield

Cammell Laird

Armour and Forgings:	Grimethorp Works, and Cyclops Works, Sheffield

ship outclassed all preceding classes of battleship, and, in effect, reduced the Royal Navy's lead in modern battleships to just one. Germany, with a formidable industrial base of its own, thus had the opportunity to keep pace with British construction. Against this background, a 'naval race' ensued between Britain and Germany, a trial of industrial strength as much as political will in which British resolve, resources and shipbuilding capacity won the day.

The Photographs

Like many shipbuilding firms, John Brown & Co used photography to record the construction of vessels, usually starting with keel laying and ending with trials. The ship's machinery, engines and boilers were also recorded. To do this, a photographic department was established at Clydebank employing up to five photographers and darkroom personnel. As this was an expensive overhead, many other shipbuilders opted to employ outside commercial firms to take progress shots as and when needed. The photographs tended to follow a similar pattern from ship to ship and established a clear record of progress at a given date. Although there was obvious interest in recording the construction of ships at Clydebank, many of which were large and prestigious, the exact purpose of the photographs is unclear. There is no evidence that they were routinely sent to ship owners and certainly no reference to them at all in correspondence with the Admiralty. Neither are they specified as a necessary part of the contract.

Presentation volumes showing the ship in various stages of construction were often given to owners on the completion of the ships, including the Admiralty. Beyond this thoughtful gesture, the photographs appear to have been for company purposes only and were often used by John Brown & Co in publicity materials and engineering articles.

That this photographic collection has survived at all the decimation that has taken place across British industry is remarkable in itself and has resulted in the preservation of one of the finest records of ship construction in modern industrial Britain. Throughout the period covered by this book, photographic exposures were made on glass plate negatives measuring 10 x 12in and occasionally on plates of 12 x 15in. The cameras used were necessarily large, and together with substantial tripods, made for a cumbersome and heavy load to be carried across the large area of a shipyard. Setting up to make an exposure was a time consuming event not to mention a hazardous and often high-wire activity given the need to climb cranes or scale hulls in various stages of completion in a dangerous working environment. Slow emulsions required time exposures which account for the sometimes blurred appearance of men working but compensated by allowing for images of exceptional detail. The growing use of photography at Clydebank can be seen in the number of exposures made for the five ships that make up this book: around sixty negatives were exposed covering the construction of *Inflexible*, rising to over 600 for *Hood*.

The first three ships, *Inflexible*, *Australia* and *Tiger*, were built under peacetime conditions where the due and lengthy process of tendering applied and no undue pressure was made on the shipbuilder during construction. This was in stark contrast to the urgency of wartime conditions where events moved much more quickly. So fast in fact, that in the case of *Repulse*, the shipbuilder was commanded to start work more or less right away with little by way of preparations, specifications or drawings to guide the way. On his retirement from John Brown's in 1946, Sir Thomas Bell recalled the meeting that he and Alexander Gracie of Fairfield's had with Lord Fisher at Christmas 1915 in order to impress on them the urgency of building *Repulse* and *Renown* rapidly and quoting him as saying 'I am going to have these ships delivered on time and if you fail me your houses will be made a dunghill and you and your wives liquidated', adding 'I expect to hear tomorrow that you have started preparations for these ships.' The environment in which *Hood* was constructed was completely different again, subject to delay through partial redesign in the wake of the battle of Jutland and then encountering an acute shortage of labour within a shipbuilding industry that was working to capacity.

The John Brown photographs of the five battlecruisers covered by this book offer an insight into this unparalleled period of industrial endeavour particularly when it is considered that a total of fifty-one capital ships were built in British yards from *Dreadnought* in 1906 to the completion of *Hood* in 1920.

Another feature of these photographs is the depiction of the ships 'as built', with the overall balance of the design as the naval architect or constructor originally intended, unadorned by service or wartime additions. The 'as built' ship provides an interesting alternative to popular images and models of warships that favour late configurations which often depict ships after years of modifications and additions with the invariable accumulation of often ungainly clutter.

Note that the NRS photo reference numbers, where applicable, are given at the end of the captions.

Acknowledgements

I would like to thank the following persons for help in the preparation of this work: Ian Buxton and Brian Newman for reading the manuscript and Ian Sturton for kindly allowing me to use some information he uncovered in researching *Hood*'s unbuilt sisters. I am indebted to the following institutions for their help in accessing their archives:

National Maritime Museum
Historic Photographs and Ship Plans Section, National Maritime Museum, Greenwich, London.
Jeremy Michel and Andrew Choong.

Glasgow University Archive Services
The Customer Services Team

National Records of Scotland
Image Library:
Matthew Fawcett, Leanne Jobling, Gill Mapstone, John Simmons, Pat Todd

Conservators:
Eva Martinez Moya, Linda Ramsay

Digital Services:
Paul Riley

A debt of thanks is also due to Rob Gardiner at Seaforth for his enthusiasm and assistance and to Stephen Dent for the design of this book.

Ian Johnston,
March 2011

SHIP No.374
INFLEXIBLE

The first reference to the *Invincible* class contained within the Ship's Cover is in a letter dated 20 March 1905, in which the Director of Naval Construction (DNC), Sir Philip Watts, was advised that the Board of Admiralty had approved the outline design submitted by the Committee on Designs for new cruisers to be included in the programme for 1905–6. The letter requested that the complete design should now be worked out and that the cruisers would be built by contract meaning by private shipyards and not by Royal Dockyards. As a new class of ship known from 1912 onwards as battlecruisers, they were at first referred to under several names such as armoured cruisers or large armoured vessels.

At Clydebank, the first reference to the contract that would become *Inflexible* was made on 16 August 1905 when the Shipyard Director, John Dunlop, reported to his board that the company was in discussion with the Admiralty concerning a large armoured vessel. At this meeting, Dunlop said that should this order proceed, a large investment in plant would be made at the yard totalling £60,000. At the same meeting, the Board took notice of the implications of the Official Secrets Act (1889) in relation to this vessel. A set of drawings and a detailed specification provided by the Admiralty formed the basis on which the shipbuilder would estimate the building costs necessary to submit a tender. Three ships of the *Invincible* class were to be constructed originally to be named *Invincible*, *Immortalité* and *Raleigh*. Of the three, it had already been decided that one (*Raleigh*) was to be fitted with electrically-operated 12in main armament mountings while her sister-ships had the proven hydraulic type as fitted in the *Lord Nelson* class pre-dreadnought battleships.

On 12 October 1905, John Brown & Co submitted a tender to the Admiralty for 'An armoured vessel to be fitted with turbines of 41,000ihp and 31 Yarrow boilers'.

	Estimate (£)	Profit (7.5%) (£)	Price (£)
1. Hull (complete)	478,000	35,850	513,850
2. Main machinery	383,480	28,761	412,241
3. Aux machinery	27,264	–	27,264
4. Inclining vessel	115	–	115
5. Armour etc.	242,925	–	242,925
6. Boats	2,050		2,050
Total	**1,133,834**	**64,611**	**1,198,445**

The tender also included a price for fitting the vessels with Babcock & Wilcox boilers which cost an extra £8,660 plus £1,340 profit giving a

Right: *Inflexible*'s stern on No 2 berth shorn of all staging and ladderways shortly before launching in June 1907. This view shows the arrangement of her twin rudders, starboard shafts and stern torpedo tube.
(NRS UCS1-118-374-12)

total of £10,000 in addition to the above. This type of boiler offered advantages over the Yarrow type but was more expensive and weighed more. Delivery of the ship on the Clyde was to be in two-and-a-half years with an additional six weeks extra for the completion of drawings.

The above tender shows the way in which the shipbuilder categorised the work to be done and estimated the cost for each category and added a profit, in this case 7.5 per cent, to give a final price. Usually, the cost for armour and armament was not given as these items were supplied to the shipbuilder by the Admiralty. In the case of *Inflexible*, a price for armour is included with no profit shown but armament is not included. The final price indicated, £1,198,445 was therefore not the final price of the vessel but the amount the shipbuilder was owed for the work done.

At the monthly Board meeting on 18 October 1905 at Clydebank, it was announced that the contract for the armoured cruiser had been won and the ship given the number 374. However this almost certainly meant that the contract was on a provisional basis. Before the contract could be awarded formally, the merits of the tender were examined and evaluated in detail by the Admiralty, resulting in a series of issues relevant to each builder and upon which final confirmation of the contract would be dependent. To give some indication of this evaluation process the following quotes have been taken from a document that was circulated around the various technical departments at the Admiralty.

Messrs Armstrong and Messrs Fairfield consider the total weight and space of the machinery sufficient and that the capacity of the boilers will give the required power. Messrs Brown do not mention this, but the total estimated weights filled in the machinery specifications by that firm agree with the specified weights, and they have submitted drawings showing the machinery in the assigned place except that:

a) the wings in the engine rooms are shown entirely cut away between stations 169 and 179.
b) recessing is shown in the middle strake of inner bottom.

If this firm's tender be accepted, submit to inform them with regard to a) and b) that the cutting away of wings and the recessing referred to, cannot be accepted.

Neither of the firms tendering propose departure from the Admiralty's design and specification of the machinery, but Messrs Brown propose some slight rearrangement of some of the auxiliary machinery in the engine rooms and alterations in the vertical position of the forward boilers. If this firm's tender be accepted, it is considered that this, subject to the remarks on the preceding paragraph, could be satisfactorily arranged.

If the Elswick tender be accepted, the firm should be informed that the 12" gun mountings, forward capstans and boat hoists are to be worked electrically in the ship to be built by them and that the necessary modifications to the ship are shown by fly tracings to the building drawings and by the accompanying revised specifications.

This evaluation shows a degree of latitude in the design and specification supplied by the Admiralty to the shipbuilder but equally, that certain elements of the design were not negotiable. In other words, while the ships would look similar and achieve similar performance levels, there would be detail differences peculiar to the approach taken by individual shipbuilders. This process of examining the tender docu-

ments in detail and discussing same with the shipbuilders took some time to complete and at November's Board Meeting at Clydebank, it was noted that they (John Brown & Co) had agreed to all of the conditions stipulated in a recent letter from the Admiralty. At December's meeting it was noted that 'the formal contract for No 374 was still not signed' and it was not until the Board meeting of 31 January 1906 that Dunlop was able to state categorically that the contract had been officially signed. This action was accompanied by the transfer of a full set of drawings to the shipbuilder to enable him to begin work. With this prestigious and profitable contract secured, the Company authorised the capital expenditure on the works to improve the level of facilities in the yard. The single most important item was the construction of a second 150-ton fitting-out crane to further enhance fitting-out arrangements in the yard – one had been ordered and erected two years earlier to fit out *Lusitania*.

On 2 December 1905, the Admiralty decided that the contracts for the ships, now given more familiar names, would be awarded. As was customary, an Admiralty representative, a constructor from the DNC's office, was appointed to each shipyard to oversee construction of the hull. Visits to the yard would also be made by other overseers to supervise construction of the ship's machinery and the installation of electrical work etc. Ordnance and armour supervisors would also inspect work undertaken by the armament and armour manufacturers, in the case of *Inflexible*, at Barrow and Sheffield.

Invincible; Armstrong Whitworth & Co, Elswick. Admiralty Overseer G Bull.
Inflexible; John Brown & Co Ltd., Clydebank. Admiralty Overseer W H Burt.
Indomitable; The Fairfield Shipbuilding & Engineering Co Ltd., Govan. Admiralty Overseer A W Cock.

The machinery for *Inflexible* and *Indomitable* was to be constructed by their builders while that of *Invincible* by Humphrys, Tennant & Co.

The Hull Overseer fulfilled a vital role throughout the building process and was responsible for monitoring progress of construction, checking materials delivered to the yard and keeping the DNC informed of progress on a regular basis. The Admiral Superintendent for the district also played an overseeing role during construction although at a greater distance. At Clydebank, overseers were provided with their own offices and facilities and would spend time working in the Admiralty Drawing Office, other shipyard departments and outside at the building berth.

As three shipyards were involved in building three ships of the *Invincible* class, the opportunity was taken to minimise the duplication of drawing office work at each yard. At the end of December 1905, the Admiralty wrote to each of the three shipyards specifying the area of the ship each would be responsible for.

This division of drawing office work reveals that most of the structural work for the hull went to Armstrong Whitworth, with most of the work associated with the armour going to Fairfield.

With orders now formally placed, in January, Fairfield wrote to the Controller requesting information on the ship's scheme of complement as 'so much depends on this'. Admiralty response was to provide Fairfield with a full list of the ships complement.

Once drawing office work began, drawings could be made available to the mould loft to enable the ship's lines to be laid off in full size.

Left: Looking forward from the quarterdeck towards 'X' turret with 'Q' turret visible on the starboard beam. A light steel blast screen has been fitted around the two 4in guns on top of 'X' turret. 'A' turret was given a similar screen although they appear to have been removed soon after. (NRS UCS1-118-374-21)

Right: John Brown also built many of the ship's boats. This view shows a completed 50ft steam pinnace for *Inflexible* sitting on blocks having been freshly painted. *Inflexible* is visible in the fitting-out basin at the left. The steel structure behind the pinnace is the lower part of the new 150-ton cantilever crane. (NRS UCS1-118-374-17)

Below: A cluttered quarterdeck in this June 1908 time exposure with naval and shipyard personnel working to complete the ship during the trials period. The ship is lying at the 'Tail of the Bank' off Greenock. (NRS UCS1-118-374-20)

Below: *Inflexible*'s conning tower and bridge structure with canvas screens in place. Skylights, hatches and lockers await fitting while worker's jackets hang on convenient items. Note the light steel screens that have been lowered to reveal a 4in gun.
(NRS UCS1-118-374-23)

Above: A midships view taken in the fitting-out basin prior to the start of trials. Apart from minor fitting-out details the ship is substantially complete, although she has yet to receive her boats.
(NRS UCS1-118-374-29)

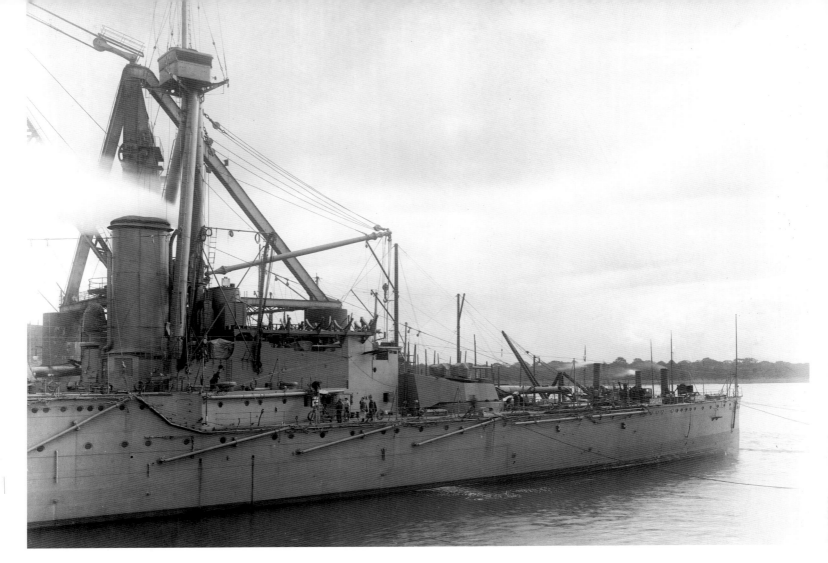

Above: The after end of the ship showing the arrangement of booms for the anti-torpedo net gear. Three tugs are waiting off *Inflexible*'s stern, possibly waiting to pull her out into the river. (NRS UCS1-118-374-30)

Right: The 12 x 10-inch plate camera used to take this photograph would have required a minor performance to set up, witnessed by the shipyard works watching intently from *Inflexible*'s bow. The ship is drawing just 23 feet forward. (NRS UCS1-118-374-28)

Below: Lying off Greenock in July 1908, this view of the midships area shows the boat stowage abaft the forward funnel. The general clutter on board indicates that this is an early trial trip to deal with any obvious difficulties after which the ship will return to the yard for completion. The paddle tug *Flying Scotsman* is alongside aft of 'P' turret. (NRS UCS1-118-374-25)

Left: A view from the forecastle deck looking aft towards 'P' turret. Note the men on top of the aftermost funnel. (NRS UCS1-118-374-24)

Right: The simplicity of the bridge and forward superstructure is evident in this view. Note how the bridge sits on the crown of the conning tower and the light supporting structure of the compass platform. (NRS UCS1-118-374-29)

Below: With the ship moored in the Firth of Clyde, workmen take a break in this view of the forecastle. Notice how far inboard the stanchions are fixed at the deck edge to allow for net stowage and the blast screens surrounding the twin 4in guns on 'A' turret. (NRS UCS1-118-374-27)

Top Left: *Inflexible*'s bow with two 125-cwt Wasteney Smith stockless anchors ready to receive a coat of paint. Not legible in this reproduction is the verse from a song painted below the staging at bottom left. It reads:

> These are the banks of Claudy
> Fair maid where on you stand
> But don't depend on Johnny
> For he's a false young man.

(NRS UCS1-118-374-31)

Top Right: It is not difficult to see how occupancy of the control tops, in this instance the after control platform, could so easily be rendered untenable by funnel smoke.
(NRS UCS1-118-374-32)

Left: The bridge, chart house and compass platform seen from the bridge wing showing a lot of canvas and wire ropes. The lower portion of a semaphore device with operating levers and chains is to the left of the tripod strut. (NRS UCS1-118-374-34)

Top: Bits of the accommodation ladder and various other items lying around on the forecastle waiting to be fitted. Note the very neat proportions of 'A' turret 12in gun house and work proceeding on the 4in guns on its roof. (NRS UCS1-118-374-35)

Bottom: 'P' turret and barbette with the associated armoured area mounted on the hull. Note the temporary cabin hoisted on board behind the turret. (NRS UCS1-118-374-29)

Above: A view of the after funnel, flying deck with boat deck above and mainmast tripod struts photographed from the roof of 'P' turret. From this image, drawings and a bowler hat can be seen in the temporary cabin denoting use by a shipyard manager or Admiralty overseer. (NRS UCS1-118-374-37)

Top right: Another view of the after superstructure and boat deck. Long davits were required to enable the 32ft life cutter to swing over the deck to the ship's side. The cast circular plates on deck are scuttles for coaling the ship. Although undated, these photographs were probably taken in June 1908. (NRS UCS1-118-374-36)

Lower right details: The ship's steam siren and access ladder mounted on a bracket secured to the rear of the forward funnel; good detail shots of a 36in searchlight and its mounting.

Left: Although the glass plate negative is cracked, at least ten ratings are visible in this photograph sleeping at their mess tables. What looks like hammocks are stowed above on the deck head. (NRS UCS1-118-374-39)

Below: A view of the refrigeration plant supplied by the Haslam Foundry & Engineering Co Ltd, Derby. The plate at the centre of the fan housing marked FAN-RR, says the fan supplies main deck cabins 34 to 55 and the forward barbette. (NRS UCS1-118-374-40)

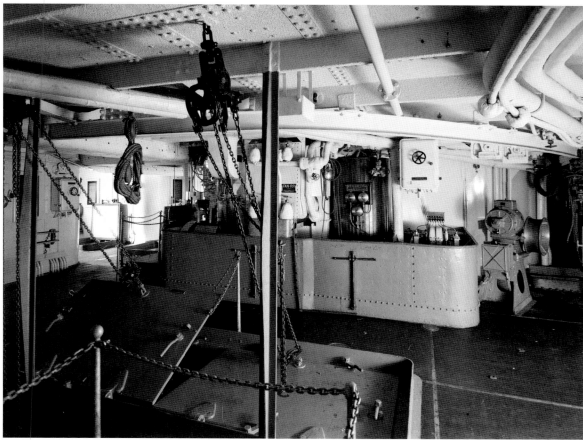

Left: A view looking forward over the 12in guns of 'P' turret with the midships boat deck at left. Note the derrick and boom for lifting the ship's boat. (NRS UCS1-118-374-38)

Right: The Admiral's Day Cabin located on the port side upper deck slightly aft of 'A' barbette. The cabin has good natural light from a large skylight as well as a window to the right. The cabin contains many personal items, some arranged on the mantle shelf and writing desk. Seven pipes have been laid out on the latter.
(NRS UCS1-118-374-42)

Left and below: Two magnificent shots of *Inflexible* steaming at full power in a calm sea displacing great troughs of sea down either side. In conditions such as these with maximum smoke being made, the after control platform would have been untenable.
Left (NRS UCS1-118-374-46)
Right (NRS UCS1-118-374-45)

Three photographs of *Inflexible* taken within a short time of one another in light condition on the Firth of Clyde during her final trials period in September 1908. She is fully rigged and all canvas screens have been fitted giving the forward superstructure a fuller look.

Top left (NRS UCS1-118-374-52)
Bottom left (NRS UCS1-118-374-49)
Right: (NRS UCS1-118-374-50)

SHIP No.402
AUSTRALIA

The battlecruisers of the *Indefatigable* class began to take shape in 1908. Conceived as slightly longer versions of the *Invincible*s, a note from the DNC dated 31 March 1908, to the Controller, John Jellicoe, the *Indefatigable* class or 'New *Invincible*s' as he referred to them, listed the difference between the new ships and the existing *Invincible* class. The approximate cost of the ships was £1,842,000. It was proposed that the machinery installation should be similar to *Invincible*.

On 24 October 1908, the Controller, John Jellicoe, wrote to the DNC, the Director of Naval Ordnance (DNO) and the Engineer-in-Chief (E-in-C) saying that it had been definitely decided that the armoured cruisers of the current year's programme (1908) should proceed and that the design should now be completed. The order for the first ship, *Indefatigable*, was placed with Devonport Dockyard. John Brown's first involvement with the ships of this class came when the order for *Indefatigable*'s machinery was placed with them because, as Jellicoe put it, 'this firm gave the lowest tender and turned out the most satisfactory machinery in *Inflexible*'.

When it became clear that the governments of Australia and New Zealand would each fund the construction of a battlecruiser, two further units were put out to tender, this time by contract, meaning that they would be built by private shipyards. Consequently, tenders were sent out to the following private firms on 23 December 1909;

Brown, Fairfield, Vickers, Palmers, Scotts, Beardmore, Cammell Laird and Harland & Wolff.
(Hull and machinery)

Armstrong Whitworth and Swan Hunter.
(Hull only)

Unlike the above yards which had associated engine works, Armstrong and Swan Hunter[1] did not which meant that the machinery for any ships they were awarded would be built elsewhere as was the case with all Dockyard built ships. Thames Ironworks was excluded from tendering on the basis of inadequate facilities.

The document sent to the shipyards inviting tenders ran to fifteen pages and set out the basic requirements to be met under a series of headings. This document was accompanied by guidance drawings, and specifications and began in the following manner:

---

[1] Swan Hunter & Wigham Richardson did have an interest in the Wallsend Slipway & Engineering Co Ltd. however.

Right: *Australia* a few days before her launch. Most of the staging has been removed from her side and the wooden ramp leading up to the deck edge will be swung out of the way. To the left, the launch platform is under erection. In the early years of the twentieth century shipbuilding berth cranes began to acquire more sophisticated characteristics as seen in this photograph where simple pole derricks arranged down either side of the building slip are being replaced by more substantial steel derricks capable of lifting 5 tons.
(NRS UCS1-118-402-50)

Gentlemen,

I am commanded by my Lords Commissioners of the Admiralty to invite you to tender for the construction and completion in all respects of the hull of an Armoured vessel for His Majesty's Navy, and also to submit with your tender a design and tender for the construction and completion in all respects of the machinery for the vessel.

2. Your tender must be delivered at the Admiralty, addressed by means of the enclosed label, not later than 12 o'clock (noon) on Friday the 29th January 1910, upon the enclosed forms, quoting separate prices for the following complete in all respects … '

The document then described hull, steering gear, main and auxiliary machinery with Yarrow boilers and alternatively with Babcock & Wilcox boilers, anchors and cables, 'Armour will be delivered by their Lordships in portions and at dates suitable for properly carrying on the

FIRST CLASS ARMOURED COLONIAL CRUISERS. 18,800 TONS AND 44,000HP.

For delivery in 24 months.

	Cost (£)	Profit (£)	Price (£)
Hull	456,500	30,700	487,200
Main machinery	232,160	29,940	262,100
Spare gear not to be carried on board:			
A) spare propeller	3,000	800	3,800
B) remainder	1,800	–	1,800
Boilers	107,470	16,730	124,200
Aux Machinery	22,750	–	22,750
Inclining	150	–	150
Total	**823,830**	**78,170**	**902,000**

For delivery in 30 months

	Cost (£)	Profit (£)	Price (£)
Hull	449,000	26,000	475,000
Main machinery	253,100	24,440	23,625
Spare gear not to be carried on board:			
A) spare propeller	3,000	800	3,800
B) remainder	1,800	–	1,800
Boilers	107,470	16,730	124,200
Aux Machinery	22,750	–	22,750
Inclining	150	–	150
Total	**815,315**	**65,485**	**880,800**

Prices finally accepted (pencil note written on above tender.)

Hull	475,015
Engines	254,632
Boilers	120,700
Aux machinery	22,650
Spares A)	3,800
Spares B)	1,800
Inclining	150
Total	**878,747**

building operations on the vessel … Gun Mountings, torpedo tubes and fittings will be supplied to you inside the periods named below …'.

Finally, a price was to be given for construction over twenty-four months and thirty months respectively. Drawings of masts, spars etc., were made available for inspection at the Admiralty between certain dates. The timescale provided for a period of less than four weeks in which the firms had to absorb the details of the design, obtain material costs and subcontractors' prices and work out their own charges – no mean feat for such large and complex vessels.

The tender submitted by John Brown & Co., dated 27 January 1910, included the following prices;

Tenders were duly received from each of the shipyards with the exception of Harland & Wolff who withdrew and the merits of each evaluated as before. This evaluation was summarised in a memo sent from the Engineer-in-Chief to the Controller on 16 February 1910. While all of the tenders were considered acceptable subject to certain conditions, the lowest tenders won and thus John Brown and Fairfield were awarded contracts.

The three ships of the *Indefatigable* class were laid down on:

Indefatigable	23 February 1909
New Zealand	20 June 1910
Australia	23 June 1910

A very long period elapsed between the construction of the first and last two ships of the class and *Indefatigable* was well on her way to completion before the other two were laid down. While the Admiralty did not make the financial gain that might have been made had all ships been built at the same time, the delay did allow some changes to be made to the design of *Australia* and *New Zealand*.

Meanwhile, in March 1910, before orders had been provisionally agreed, the Admiralty placed orders with Armstrong Whitworth and Vickers Son & Maxim for one set each of 12in 45-calibre hydraulic gun machinery and shields. This version of the 12in machinery appears to have been an Armstrong design as they were requested to provide drawings to Vickers.

On 17 March, the Admiralty telegraphed John Brown provisionally accepting their tender for the large armoured cruiser. This was followed on 1 April 1910, when letters were sent from the Contracts branch of the Admiralty to John Brown and Fairfield advising that they had been awarded contracts on a provisional basis subject to conditions.

In the case of *Australia* the letter confirmed the following prices:

Hull	£475,015
Steering gear by Messrs Davies & Co., (included in above price). £2,015	
The hull price included the cost of incandescent lamps for lighting the ship. £2,000	
Main and Auxiliary machinery	£254,632
Spare propellers one complete set	£3,800
Spare gear not be carried in the vessel	£1,800
Babcock & Wilcox boilers	£120,700
Inclining	£150
Total	**£858,097**

Delivery to be on or before 30 September 1912.

On 27 April, John Brown was advised by the Admiralty that the following items of auxiliary machinery had been approved for their ship:

Distilling machinery, G&J Weir.	£6,700
Steering engines, Napier Brothers.	£3,125
Torpedo air compressing machinery, General Engine & Boiler Co.	£1,569
Electric generating machinery, Belliss & Morcom Co.,	£3,991
Refrigerating, ice-making and magazine cooling Machinery, Pulsometer Engineering Co.	£8,200
Forward and after capstan, Harfield & Co.	£5,065
Total	**£28,650**

With the shipbuilders agreeing to meet the contract conditions, the final contract was signed initiating the flow of detailed information from the Admiralty, consisting of outline drawings and specifications. On 1 April 1910, the following drawings were forwarded to the shipyard.

Sheer
Midship Section
Rig
Armour
Profile
Boats and bridge
Flying deck
Forecastle deck
Upper deck
Main deck
Lower deck
Platforms
Hold
Sections forward
Sections aft

In addition to the above, numerous other detail drawings such as scheme of riveting, forward framing, watertight bulkheads and super-structure plating were also provided. The drawings were accompanied by specifications for the hull running to sixty-three separate sections. While these drawings encapsulated the complete design of the ship, the contractor's ship and engine drawing offices used them to develop hundreds of working drawings necessary to enable construction down to the smallest detail. On 19 April 1910, John Brown and Fairfield were informed that Admiralty overseers had been appointed to oversee construction. At Clydebank the hull overseer was C G Hall and at Fairfield, C Lillicrap. Engineer Commander W Whittingham RN, was appointed to oversee construction of the ship's machinery for *Australia* assisted by Mr W Sudweeks in overseeing the construction of her boilers.

With the shipyard now provided with sufficient information to get started, the Admiralty began to place orders for items that remained their responsibility namely, armament and armour. The 12in main armament mechanisms and turrets for *Australia* were awarded to Vickers Son & Maxim at Barrow, while the armour was spread across the main armour

plants in the UK. Thus, a stream of orders were issued for heavy armoured items, forgings and castings, including communication tubes, bulkhead plates, ammunition trunks, belt and barbette armour.

With *Indefatigable* well advanced, and *New Zealand* at much the same stage of construction as *Australia*, there was a considerable volume of traffic between the three shipbuilders as well as with the Admiralty and its suppliers. The following letters, originating at Clydebank from August to October 1910, are indicative of communications and demonstrate the close collaboration that took place.

Letter to Armstrong Whitworth, Elswick. Plans and drawings etc., are being put on express train from Glasgow to arrive Newcastle later today.

11 August acknowledging drawing showing stump mast on *Indefatigable* and sea cocks on that ship which we propose to adopt for *Australia*.

17 August. Letter thanking Fairfield for drawings of anchor and cable arrangements for *Indefatigable*. Also forwarding details to Fairfield for shell room gear as per drawings of *Indefatigable*.

17 August. Letter to Fairfield attaching drawings showing arrangement of Dispensary and Poison Cupboard on HMS *St Vincent* which Clydebank will adopt for *Australia*.

18 August. Letter acknowledging ten tracings from Fairfield showing details of coaling winches which Fairfield had received from W H Allen Son & Co.

24 August. Letter noting the return of tracings to Fairfield showing details of stiffening plates on brackets on bulkhead for main steam pipes.

1 September. Letter to Armstrong Whitworth, Openshaw Works, Manchester, concerning the order for belt armour and barbette armour for P & Q turrets. This was accompanied by drawings showing bolt holes and small holes for the face of the plates.

Another letter of same date advises that a railway wagon with moulds has been dispatched from Clydebank with 139 moulds for plates 23 and 4 to 63 and 4 inclusive and also for erection moulds for plates 1 & 2 and 29 & 30.

9 September. Letter to Cammell Laird, Sheffield, providing a drawing with details of communication tubes. On the same date, a letter to Cammell Laird giving details of armoured bolts for the side armour.

15 September. Letter to Fairfield regarding 'Colonial Cruisers' and thanking them for supply of drawings of rudder cross heads and rigging plan.

Letter of same date to Fairfield saying that Clydebank is working on plans for the steam disinfector which should be available soon. Also plans for submerged torpedo arrangements will be available in three to four weeks. The plan of stools for doubling plates on Platform Deck is almost complete.

20 October. Letter to Armstrong Whitworth, Openshaw, Manchester.

'Cruiser AUSTRALIA No 402.

With reference to your letter of 13th inst., asking for sketch showing tap holes in face of 200lbs belt armour plates, we may state that the details for these plates are being prepared (by mutual consent) by Messrs The Fairfield Co. These friends inform us that we will be in a position to give full particulars of the bolt holes of the 160 and 200 lbs belt armour early next week, and trusting that this will be satisfactory to you.'

Any attempt on the part of the shipbuilder to complete construction of *Australia* on time was seriously delayed when a national lockout of boilermakers began on 3 September 1910 lasting until mid December. The boilermakers, who made up the principal steelworking trades, were by far the most significant at this stage of construction and this action on the part of the employers, who were in dispute with the Boilermaker's Society over procedural agreements, resulted in little or no progress for three and a half months. Labour shortages then conspired to delay *Australia* further and in March the shipyard noted that progress on her hull was not satisfactory owing to the scarcity of men. The result was that *Australia* was not launched until 25 October 1911, almost four months after *New Zealand* had been launched at Fairfield. Her displacement at launching draught was 7,110 tons while the weight of her hull was 5,754.8 tons. In a further effort to speed completion of *Australia*, management switched men to her from the cruiser *Southampton* which had been laid down in September.

In 1911, while Clydebank management did what they could to make up lost time, the new Official Secrets Act was passed in the House of Commons prompting the Admiralty to write to shipbuilders in May reminding them of the need to ensure secrecy in Admiralty work 'in order that the public interest may be served' noting that failure to do so would bar them from future tenders.

In early January 1912, work on *Australia*'s main armament at Barrow was well advanced with pit trials of 'A' and 'P' mountings about to start. However, serious delays in the supply of her armour, especially barbette armour, compounded existing delays resulting in *Australia* remaining in the shipyard for considerably longer than the original completion date of September 1912. This was a serious issue for the shipbuilder who complained that the vessel will now take up 'valuable room in our dock

AUSTRALIA: TRIAL CONDITION

	Tons
Weight of ship on 14 January 1913	15,860
Weight to come off, plant, excess water in boilers etc	208
Weight to complete hull and machinery	248
Load for trial:	
Coal, across several bunkers	1,370
Reserve feed water	480
Water ballast	860
Fresh water	135
Water in hydraulic tanks	55
Men and effects	80
Stores etc.	140
Displacement	19,020

for 18 months instead of the 11 anticipated'. The National Coal Strike which began at the end of February lasting for six weeks imposed further delays. It was not until January 1913 that the ship was sufficiently complete that preparation for trials could begin.

On 17 February, the ship left Clydebank to carry out preliminary trials on the Firth of Clyde. By March, the main trials programme was underway with preliminary trials of her hydraulic main armament gun mechanisms followed by machinery trials on the measured mile off Polperro. These trials began with the 30 hours 3/5ths power trials on 7/8 March. Six runs were successfully completed and it was noted that *Australia* was 0.5 knot slower than *New Zealand* at the same power but that coal consumption was rather less.

On 11 March, full power trials were run on the Polperro mile at which *Australia* managed a mean speed of 26.89 knots developing 55,881shp. On the fastest of four runs, she made 27.482 knots on 56,050shp. The wind was SW, force 4–2, sea smooth. The ship drew 26ft forward and 27ft aft. The mean high power of 55,880shp was 27 per cent in excess of the designed full power and the same as achieved in *Indefatigable*. On her return to Clydebank, she was inclined on 17 May 1913, departing for torpedo trials on 10 June. On 18 June, *Australia* left Clydebank to complete her trials finally sailing on 20 June for Portsmouth where she was commissioned the following day as flagship of the Royal Australian Navy.

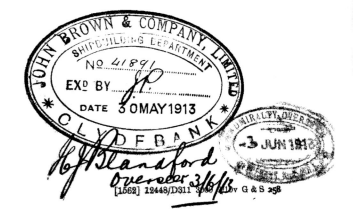

Great volumes of documentation passed both ways between the Admiralty and shipbuilder during construction, most of which were stamped and countersigned. The stamps shown here are from documents created during the final stages of *Australia*'s construction and trials period.

Above: *Australia*'s twin rudder and shaft arrangements were very similar to *Inflexible*'s, although the stern torpedo tube had been dispensed with. Note the recess for the armoured belt and the close proximity of *Australia* to the ship under construction on the berth to the right. Although they are standing a slight distance behind the port rudder, the three men dressed in white aprons to the left of the rudder give some indication of scale. (NRS UCS1-118-402-49)

Above: *Australia* was launched on 25 October 1911. Here, guests are assembling for the launch. Members of the public attending the launch were retained behind the fence at right. (NRS UCS1-118-402-59)

Left: *Australia* being prepared for launching. The ship is still resting on keel blocks, which can be seen under her bow. Her weight will shortly be transferred to the poppets, one of which can be seen here. Bunting is being rigged while the large metal boxes in the foreground have been used to lift scrap materials or tools off the ship. (NRS UCS1-118-402-56)

Right: The forward poppet on the port side. Poppets were constructed from massive baulks of pitch pine, tied together and held in position by steel framing riveted to the ship's side. Poppets, two at the stern and two at the bow, supported the ship's weight on the sliding ways which ran down the slipways which were lubricated with soap and tallow. Drag chains bundled on the ground are connected to temporary fittings on the ship's side by wire ropes seen here hanging loosely. (NRS UCS1-118-402-53)

Above: The ship in the river surrounded by debris. The space where the six-inch side armour will be fitted can be clearly seen. (NRS UCS1-118-402-63)

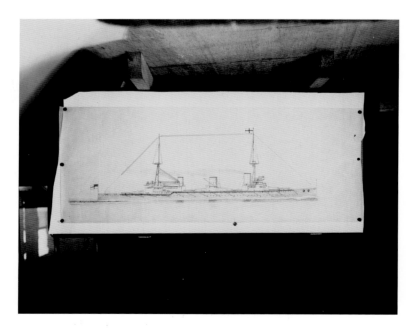

Left: A simple pen and wash sketch of rig which the shipbuilder photographed for reasons unknown as far more detailed formal drawings were in existence. (NRS UCS1-118-402-64)

Right: *Australia* brought to a halt only 70 to 80 feet from the end of the launching ways. The debris at the end of the ways and in the water is timber from the sliding ways and poppets which has floated off. The ship was launched by Florence Reid, wife of the Australian High Commissioner and former Prime Minister, Sir George Reid. (NRS UCS1-118-402-62)

Above: *Australia* at her fitting-out berth by the 150-ton cantilever crane where she would remain for nineteen months. Funnels, masts, belt armour and much of her superstructure are in place. The booms for the anti-torpedo net defence are being rigged. (NRS UCS1-118-402-66)

Left: Work has progressed on the bridge since the preceding photograph. An *Acheron* class destroyer, either *Hornet* or *Hydra* is fitting out alongside. Pontoons were used for a variety of purposes down the ship's side. The pontoon at left with rotary air pump was used to support a diver who inspected the hull for obstructions and to remove redundant fittings etc. (NRS UCS1-118-402-65)

Right: In this wider view of the fitting-out basin the cruiser *Southampton* is at right alongside SS *Niagra* for the New Zealand line. An *Acheron* class destroyer is alongside *Australia* while another destroyer can be seen under construction by the covered berth off to the right. *Australia* is very light as none of her 12in mountings have been fitted. There are no pictures of these mountings being lifted into the ship. (NRS UCS1-118-402-91)

Above: Looking over the conning tower (and showing how the armoured hatch operated) and 'A' turret to the forecastle cluttered with ropes of various sizes. *Aquitania* is fitting-out at the other side of the fitting-out basin with *Emperor Peter the Great* for the Russian Steam Navigation Co in between. (NRS UCS1-118-403-676)

Left: *Australia* getting ready to leave Clydebank in this impressive view of 'P' turret and its 12in guns. Two painters are applying finishing touches underneath. The railway coaches brought into the yard at right have probably delivered the ship's crew from Portsmouth, Devonport or Chatham while the private car by the companionway suggests the arrival of a senior officer. *Aquitania*'s stern can be seen at left. (NRS UCS1-118-402-69)

Right: Various details, including watertight doors, mushroom vents, ladderways, booms, stanchions and coaling scuttles, are evident in this shot on the forecastle deck looking forward. Rain has darkened the decks. (NRS UCS1-118-402-68)

Left: Looking forward to 'Y' turret and the after superstructure. The ship's crew, some dressed in whites, are familiarising themselves with their ship. With the exception of one man at left, the photographer is being watched intently. (NRS UCS1-118-402-70)

Right: A detail of the after boat deck with an Admiral's barge and steam pinnace sitting on their cradles. (NRS UCS1-118-402-74)

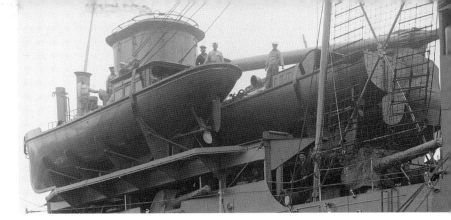

Below: Looking aft towards the middle funnel, boat deck and 'Q' turret. The relatively uncluttered area of deck was necessary so that 'P' turret could fire across the beam. (NRS UCS1-118-402-72)

Left: Looking forward to 'Q' turret, the midships funnel and bridge beyond. The tangle of cables at left appears to be the ship's aerials with spreaders yet to be rigged between the masts. (NRS UCS1-118-402-73)

Below: The after superstructure with searchlight platform at top. Four 4in guns are housed in this structure, the lower two of which had an elaborate system of shutters to close them off – as shown here completely closed. (NRS UCS1-118-402-71)

Left: *Australia* has a look of imminent departure in this shot as crew and a few shipyard workers stare at the photographer. (NRS UCS1-118-402-74)

Right: The after superstructure and boat deck with 50ft steam pinnace. A 4in gun is mounted directly underneath the pinnace, all but invisible behind shutters. The cutters in stowed position by the mainmast are almost 40 feet above the quarterdeck. The crew gathered on deck are carrying kit of some sort. (NRS UCS1-118-402-75)

Below: Officers and crew gathered around the 12in guns of 'Y' turret. Turbine casings lie underneath the big crane ready for delivery to shipyards elsewhere. The West Yard covered berths are visible in the background. (NRS UCS1-118-402-76)

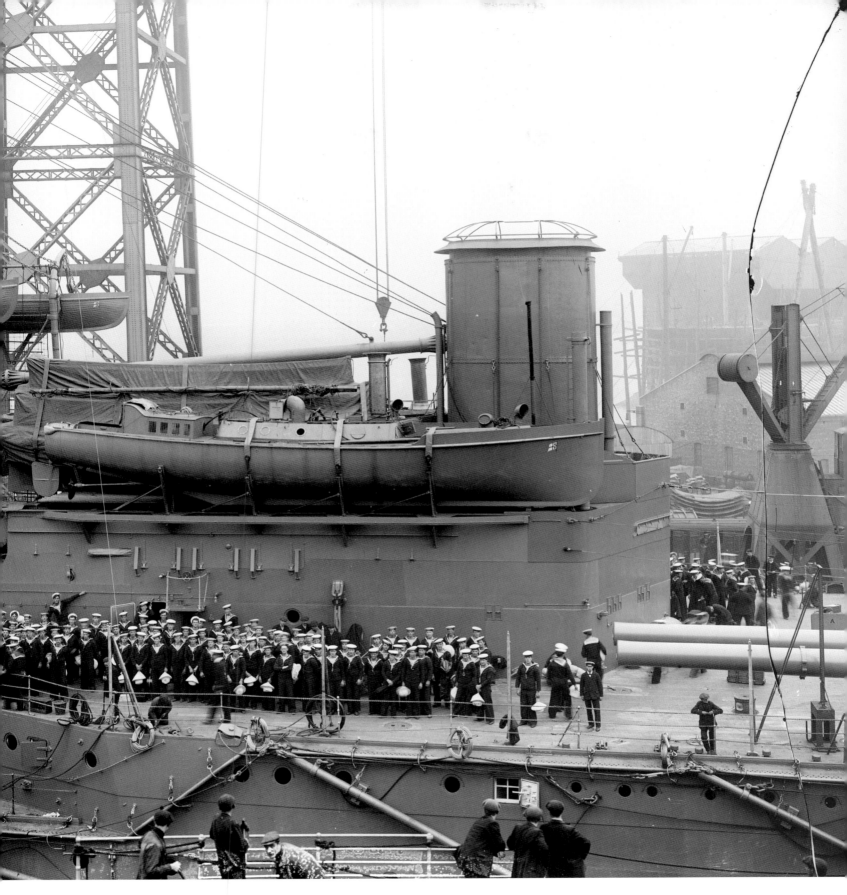

Above: A good view of 'Q' and 'P' turrets, manufactured by Vickers at Barrow, giving a good idea of the en echelon arrangement and the clear deck space required for firing across the beam. The spots are not an early form of camouflage but caused by deterioration on the glass plate negative. (NRS UCS1-118-402-77)

Left: From the same sequence as the previous shots, this photograph looks over the stern of the Russian Steam Navigation Co's *Emperor Peter the Great* to *Australia* getting ready for departure from Clydebank probably about the middle of June 1913. Note the blast bags are being fitted to the guns of 'A' turret. (NRS UCS1-118-402-79)

Right: Although structurally complete *Australia* is still waiting to take on coal and other stores and thus sitting high in the water. (NRS UCS1-118-402-82)

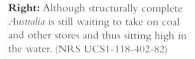

Above: Another view of the after superstructure and flying deck. (NRS UCS1-118-402-78)

Opposite: The after superstructure showing the searchlight platform with four twin 24in searchlights under covers and the boat deck with the 32ft cutters in the stowed position. (NRS UCS1-118-402-81)

Right: *Australia*'s bridgework and tall fore funnel clearing the height of the bridge and compass platform. (NRS UCS1-118-402-80)

Above, Left and Right: Three views of *Australia* at rest during trials on 18 and 19 June 1913.
(NRS UCS1-118-402-83, 85 and 87)

SHIP No.418
TIGER

Tiger, like her immediate predecessor *Queen Mary*, was a development of the *Lion* class, both ships of which were completed in 1912. The design for *Tiger* was sufficiently advanced in the last quarter of 1911 to enable tenders to be prepared and on 22 December 1911, the tender document, running to twenty-four pages of specifications, was sent to the following firms: Armstrong Whitworth; William Beardmore; John Brown; Cammell Laird; Fairfield; Palmers; Scotts; Swan Hunter; and Vickers. As with previous tender invitations, the following list of drawings was made available to the shipbuilders for tendering purposes.

Sectional drawing
Profile
Shelter deck etc.
Forecastle deck
Upper deck
Main deck
Lower deck
Platform decks
Hold
Sections forward
Sections aft
Sketch of rig

However, in a note dated 29 January 1912, sent to the E-in-C and the DNC, both were informed not to give attention to tenders from Cammell Laird, Beardmore, Scotts and Armstrong. This most probably indicates that either these firms had a sufficient volume of Admiralty work already or that a contract distribution system was in operation. On 23 January 1913, John Brown's tender was submitted at the following price:

With Babcock & Wilcox Boilers and Brown-Curtis turbines

	Cost (£)	Charges (£)	Price (£)
Hull	537,200	58,000	595,200
(including preparing the berth etc.	7,000)		
Engines	364,945	22,700	387,650
(Includes forgings	5,000)		
Boilers	124,265	5,125	129,390
Total	1,026,415	85,825	1,112,240
Extra for superheaters	7,000		

However, written in pencil beside the above are another set of figures which are most likely to be the actual figures quoted after revisions made during the tendering process. These are:

Hull	595,200
Engines	387,645
Boilers	129,390
Auxiliary Machinery	27,967
Inclining	190
Total	**1,140,392**

The price quoted with Babcock & Wilcox boilers and Parsons turbines was:

Cost (£)	Profit (£)	Price (£)
1,028,385	85,825	1,114,210

A note below this quote and added later, noted that Vickers price was £17,000 higher than John Brown's and that Fairfield's was higher again although the latter was prepared to drop the price by £20,000 if three months was added to the construction period.

With tenders submitted from the shipbuilders, the evaluation of each bid began. While tenders concentrated on aspects of the ship to be built, confidence in the plant and facilities was an important factor. Shipbuilders were required to state on what building slip the ship would be built and the distance the ship would be 'brought up in' after launch – i.e., how long was the launching run. Based on the geography of the yards concerned, the longest run was Cammell Laird who specified three-quarters of a mile into the Mersey while, in much narrower rivers, the shortest was Palmers at just 50ft with Clydebank's run at 75ft.

Of great interest to the Admiralty at this time was the Curtis turbine which had been fitted in the US battleship *North Dakota*. As early as 1907, Thomas Bell visited General Electric's works in Schenectady, New York, to meet Charles Curtis and see his turbine. In May of the following year, agreement was reached between John Brown & Co and the International Curtis Marine Turbine Company for the UK manufacturing rights. In June 1908, the Admiralty authorised the construction of a 2,500shp demonstration turbine at Clydebank the trials of which were very successful. This resulted in the Admiralty's decision to fit these turbines, now referred to as Brown-Curtis turbines, in the 'Town' class cruisers *Bristol* and *Yarmouth*. Brown's tender for *Tiger*, offered Brown-Curtis turbines as well as the Parsons type. This proposal was well

Right: Taken on 5 December 1913, just ten days before launch, this photograph gives some indication of the density of timber staging around the hull. (NRS UCS1-118-418-54)

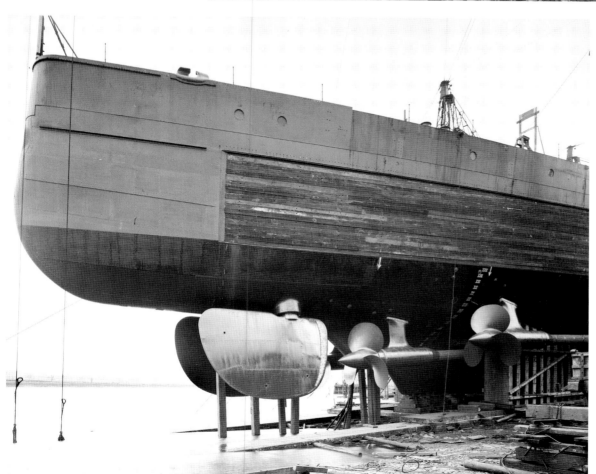

Left: Eight days later, 13 December, the staging has gone and *Tiger*'s propellers have been fitted. The recessed area lined with timber is where the belt armour will be fitted, in this instance right aft to protect the steering gear. The horizontal section of angle iron extending from the end of the armour recess to the stern is where the sternwalk will later be fitted. (NRS UCS1-118-418-44)

Below: 15 December 1913, the day of her launch. Her bow is now supported by the poppet, all keel blocks having been removed. (NRS UCS1-118-418-48)

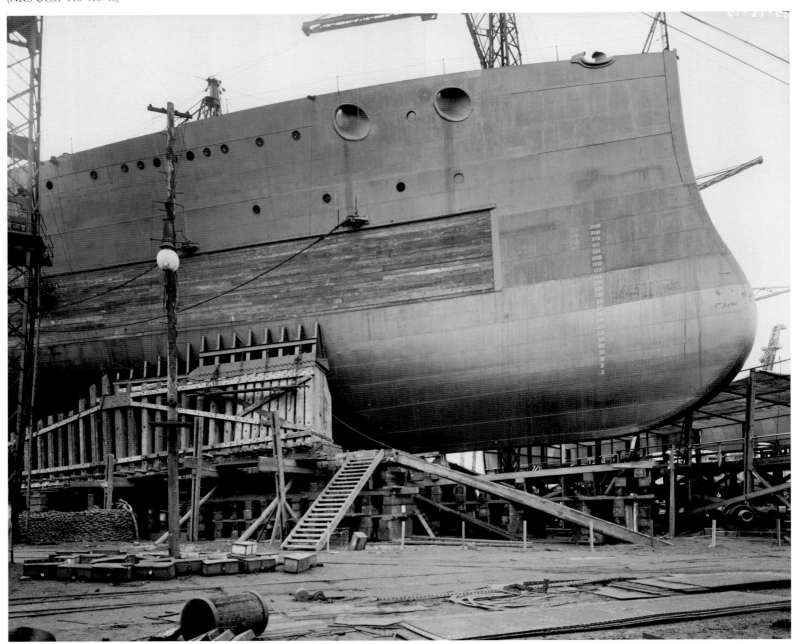

received and considered to be a 'decided advantage'. In referring this to the Controller said it was noted that John Brown's tender had provided for a 25 per cent overload over the specified 75,000shp, that is, for 93,000shp with provision for a further increase in power. This power was to be obtained in an engine room 12ft shorter than that for the Parsons design of 75,000shp. The note continued 'that this reduction in length of engine space is very large, viz, about 10?% and the saving in a new design would be very valuable. It is also accompanied by a considerable saving in weight.' The use of Brown-Curtis turbines coupled to Brown's price, probably secured the contract for them. On 2 March 1912, the Admiralty telegraphed John Brown advising that they had provisionally won the contract. On 3 April, this was followed by a letter:

Gentlemen,

In confirmation of Admiralty telegram of 2 March 1912, I am commanded by my Lords Commissioners of the Admiralty to acquaint you that, subject to your acceptance of the conditions hereinafter enumerated, they are pleased to accept your tender, dated the 23 January 1912, to construct, complete in all respects and deliver at the nearest open water to the port of construction, a battlecruiser, HMS Tiger, for HM Royal Navy with Brown-Curtis turbines and Babcock & Wilcox boilers, in accordance with the conditions and documents upon which you tendered, for the total sum of £1,112,425 … Delivery on or before 31st March 1914.

Watching events from the other side of the Atlantic, Charles Curtis wrote to an employee, Stephen Pigott, who had been sent as his representative to Clydebank:

I am requested by the directors of our company to say that they wish to congratulate you most heartily on the admirable work you have been doing on behalf of the John Brown company, but which has resulted largely for the benefit of our company, and particularly to congratulate you for getting the award for the large battleship cruiser the references to which we saw in the papers here some weeks ago. The directors all think as I do, that your work and the part you have played in the matter has shown not only excellent engineering ability, but has shown tact and capacity to deal with practical matters and with individuals under very difficult conditions.

There were difficulties, American turbines, after all, had been selected for Britain's newest and largest warship. When it became clear that under the terms of John Brown's licence agreement with Parsons they had to pay Parsons a royalty for any turbine they manufactured, including the Curtis type, Charles Curtis reacted as this would make his turbine more expensive. In response to this, Thomas Bell, managing director at Clydebank, wrote the following revealing but firm reply:

… as regards paying royalties to Parsons, I would tell you for your private information, that people in high positions in the British Navy were so impressed with the wonderful additional tactical advantages obtained in ships fitted with turbines and oil fired boilers that they felt a big debt of gratitude to Sir Charles Parsons, and I was given to understand that if we agreed to pay Parsons' turbine royalty

HMS TIGER: ARMOUR CONTRACTORS

Date	Supplier	Armour
1912		
2 May	Cammell Laird	Armoured bulkheads
5 June	Wm Beardmore	Forward & after 4in communication tubes
1 July	Vickers	Belt armour
7 July	John Brown	'A' barbette
5 June	Hadfield Steel Foundry	Forward 3in communication tube
31 May	John Brown	Gun hoists 'A' and 'B' barbettes 'X' barbette
12 July	John Brown	'B' barbette
12 July	Vickers	Belt armour
25 July	John Brown	'Q' barbette
21 November	John Brown	Battery and casemate armour
23 December	Beardmore John Spencer & Son Ltd Steel Co of Scotland Colvilles.	High tensile steel casemates and battery
1913		
16 April	Cammell Laird	Torpedo control tower (walls & floors)
2 June	Thomas Firth	Roof plate to control tower
9 December	Armstrongs	Conning tower armour
1914		
5 January	Edgar Allen & Co.	Torpedo control tower

during the continuance of our license, whether the turbines were his or other types, all opposition would be withdrawn to the introduction of your turbine into the British Navy. In view of this, and also the fact that our Company was not prepared to carry out a wearisome and expensive law suit with the Parsons Company over the matter, we thought it well to agree, and I am sure you will not be the losers by this.

With the contract for Tiger now placed and the issue of her propulsion settled, the contract assumed a familiar pattern. In April, Admiralty overseers were appointed, L D Stansfeld as Hull Overseer and Engineering Commander W F Hinchcliff to oversee the manufacture and installation of machinery and boilers.

On 15 April 1912 the Admiralty wrote to Clydebank authorising the following suppliers of auxiliary machinery:

Distilling machinery. Messrs Weir Ltd. £7,600
Steering engines. Messrs Napier Bros. £2,650
Steering wheels and telemotors. Napier Bros. £720
Air compressing machinery. P Brotherhood & Co. £3,480
Electric generator driven by steam reciprocating engine. Brewett,
Lindley & Co. with dynamos by Rees Roturbo Co. £1,503
Electric generators driven by oil reciprocating engines.
Thornycroft & Co with dynamos by Rees Roturbo Co. £3,455

Electric generators driven by turbines and dynamos.
   British Thomson Houston Co.   £4,312
Refrigerating & magazine cooling machinery. Haslan Foundry Co.
                                               £3,447
After capstan machinery. Clarke Chapman & Co.   £800

Prices for *Tiger*'s main armament hydraulic mountings had already been obtained from Armstrongs and Vickers at £238,499 and £237,781 respectively with the order going to the latter and a delivery date of June 1913 specified. From May 1912 onwards, a series of contracts were issued by the Director of Navy Contracts to armour manufacturers with delivery timed for the ship at the appropriate point. Each contract was accompanied by a drawing of the armour as rolled and as in the case of the contract to Cammell Laird for armoured bulkheads for example, specified the weight of plate, the bulkhead to which it would be attached, the ballistic requirements of the plate, price per ton and date of delivery. All deliveries were to be made to the Hull Overseer at Clydebank.

Apart from the rejection of two shaft brackets which showed hairline cracks and had to be recast, progress on *Tiger* ran smoothly and she was launched by Lady Helen Vincent on 15 December 1913 at a weight of 13,000 tons. The ship was taken into the fitting-out basin where the Cunard liner *Aquitania*, launched the previous April, was also fitting out. Although *Tiger* would be the largest ship so far built for the Royal Navy at 28,500 displacement tons and 704ft overall, she was dwarfed by *Aquitania* at 45,000 gross tons and 901ft. As the men of the fitting-out trades began work on *Tiger*, at Barrow, Vickers were making good progress with 'Q' and 'X' turrets both of which completed successful pit trials in January 1914, albeit six months late. 'A' turret followed in March and 'B' in April. In February, the Admiralty decided that *Tiger* would be fitted but not stored as a flagship.

With a huge fleet at sea during this period, a wealth of information on the design of ships was constantly being fed back to the Admiralty who would naturally make changes to ships under construction or inform the design process generally. The principal alterations made to *Tiger*'s design since August 1912 are given here:

Re-arrangement of cabins, messes, etc., in order to berth most of the men on upper deck in daylight and give crew twenty-two inches per man seating accommodation.
Additional lights and vents to living spaces.
WC added near compass platform.
Position of torpedo control tower altered.
Wheels for working magazine flood valve grouped in watertight cabinets on main deck.
Bilge keels deepened amidships.
Increased number of pneumatic tubes for transmission of messages. (This item was subsequently scored through in pencil.)
Struts added to foremast and mast shifted further forward on account of director firing.
Steering engines removed from transverse bulkhead.
Police office added.
Cable lockers made smaller.
New arrangement of coding office, signal distributing office and intelligence office etc.
Modification to gun control tower to put control officer in fixed portion.

Hawse pipe added for stern anchor.

Steel lockers for men's clothes substituted for bags and racks.

Armour gratings of cast steel instead of being built up.

Thin wood backing added behind battery armour.

Anti-aircraft guns and ammunition added for same.

Boats fitted on shelter deck instead of on forecastle deck.

Larger silent cabinet fitted in WT office.

Fifty-gallon fresh water tank added in bakery.

Oil fuel filling arrangements largely increased because of large quantity of oil carried.

Torpedo net defences abolished.

Additional baths in officers' bathrooms.

Position of searchlights altered.

Dirty clothes lockers added for POs and seamen's wash places.

Number of 3pdr guns reduced from six to four.

Separate fan and heater for drying room.

Modification to ventilation based on Ventilation Committee's First Interim Report.

Two 5-ton portable pumps in lieu of one 10-ton.

Two officers' 6in control hoods added.

In June 1914, the shipbuilders were asked to quote for manning *Tiger* with a civilian crew during her trials period. Presumably this indicated that navy personnel were preoccupied in preparing for the summer test mobilisation given the looming international crisis. The prices given were as follows:

To man the hull   £10,300 (including charges and profit)
To man the machinery   £30,460 (including charges and profit at
                                                        33 per cent)
Grades of men:
Hull: 110 sailors, 15 shipwrights, 20 others.   145 men
Machinery: 460 stokers and trimmers, record party 105 men.   565 men
Total   710 men
Number of days: 36 days from leaving Clydebank until return including 23 days of trials.

Whether or not the Admiralty accepted this is unclear.

When the war broke out in August, great efforts were made to complete *Tiger* as quickly as possible by working all available hours on extended overtime and night shifts. With this push, *Tiger* was able to commission at Clydebank on 4 October 1914, leaving the yard on the same day. Steam trials were carried out on 12 October on the Polperro

mile with the ship developing a mean of 104,635shp on full power for 29 knots at 278.3 revolutions. *Tiger's* gunnery trials were successfully conducted in October. The firing programme for 'A' turret was typical for the other three, all of which fired to starboard excepting 'B' turret which fired to port.

'A' TURRET FIRING PROGRAMME

Round	Gun	Charge	Elevation	Bearing	Recoil	Remarks
1	R	Reduced	horizontal	60° stbd	34.6"	
2	L	"	"	80° "	32.6"	
3	R	Full	5°	80° "	40.0"	
4	L	"	"	100° "	35.1"	
5	R	"	Extreme elevation	110° "	41.8"	Flat-nosed
6	L	"	"	120° "	37.6"	Flat-nosed
7	R	"	Extreme depression	120° "	40.9"	Simultaneous packed back
8	L	"	"	120° "	37.7"	"

While 'A' and 'X' turrets appeared to work without mishap, it was noted that 'Q' turret had been unable to fire rounds 7 and 8 simultaneously as intended because the left gun misfired due to the interceptor not being properly made. Additionally, on the left gun, the gun-loading cage would not come right up without assistance by lowering the breech of the gun. A comment for 13.5in guns stated that: 'The air pipe blast pipe on the gun [one] became displaced when the gun ran out. Damage to the interceptor was only avoided by one of the gun's crew bearing against the pipe as the gun ran out. An extra clip on the end ring near breech hinge pin is required.' Each 6in gun was fired four times at a range of elevations and bearings.

The estimated cost of *Tiger* at the design stage was £2,209,000 broken down as:

Hull and equipment	£697,000
Armour	£435,000
Machinery	£592,000
Gun mountings	£331,000
Guns and torpedo tubes	£154,000

John Brown's portion of the above costs (hull and machinery) was £1,289,000, and in excess of their January 1913 estimate of £1,112,240 by £176,760.

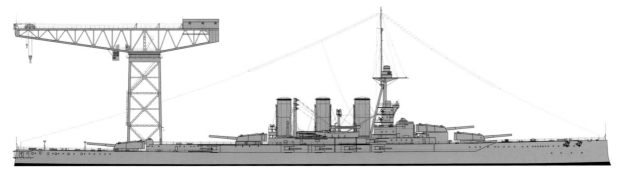

Left: *Tiger* drawn in scale to the 150-ton giant cantilever crane used to fit her out. This crane was required to lift heavy items such as turbines, boilers, condensers, main armament mountings and guns etc. Although the battlecruisers have long gone, as has John Brown's shipyard, the crane remains as a visitor attraction. (Drawing by the author)

Above: This view taken on 17 February 1914 shows *Tiger* lying at the west wharf in the fitting-out basin. A derrick crane has been positioned on deck to assist in completing the openings of 'A' and 'B' barbettes prior to shipping the roller paths and gun machinery. Note the extensive wood lined area on the hull where the side armour will be fitted. The West Yard steel working sheds and covered slipways are in the background. (NRS UCS1-118-418-82)

Left: One of the LP rotors for *Tiger* receiving its blades in the erecting shop at Clydebank on 17 December 1913. In the foreground at right are four of the main bearings for this turbine, with two other bearings for another turbine. (NRS UCS1-118-418-62)

Above: Although the largest warship so far built for the Royal Navy, *Tiger* is
dwarfed by the Cunard liner *Aquitania* in this view taken on 5 May 1914. *Aquitania*
left Clydebank to run trials five days later. Armour has been fitted to 'A' and 'B'
barbettes and also the conning tower. Note the armoured communications tube in
the forward part of the conning tower. (NRS UCS1-118-418-85)

Right: 11 June 1914. Armoured gratings and the wheels from large centrifugal fans
lying near 'Q' barbette awaiting fitting. 'Q' barbette comprises twelve curved 8-9in
thick armoured plates jointed together by the tongued and grooved method. These
plates were manufactured at John Brown's Atlas Works in Sheffield and brought to
Clydebank by train. Planking has begun on the forecastle. (NRS UCS1-118-418-88)

Left: Another view taken on 17 August. *Tiger* is substantially complete, the only obviously major items not yet fitted being the forward 6in guns and the revolving main armament director on the conning tower. (NRS UCS1-118-418-101)

Right: 25 August. *Tiger* is heavily cluttered in this view looking aft over the funnels to 'P' and 'Y' turrets. The quarterdeck has been planked and work planking the forecastle deck is all but complete. The boat deck has a corticene covering. The ship has been pushed out from the dock to allow work on the 6in guns to proceed. (NRS UCS1-118-418-110)

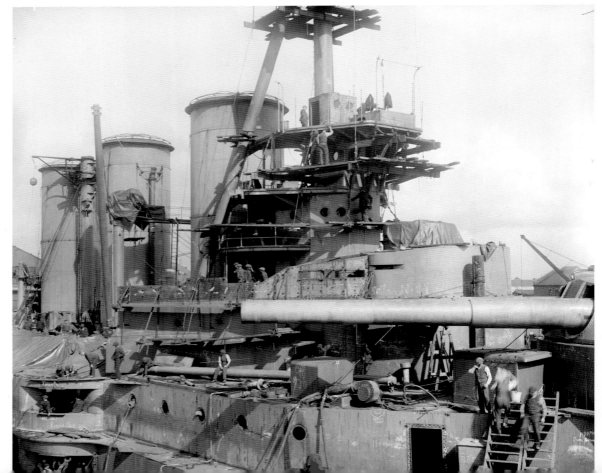

Right: In this view taken on 25 August, the twin 13.5in guns of 'B' turret loom over the shelter deck. Someone has painted 'River Bar' over No 1 gun embrasure. (NRS UCS1-118-418-109)

Left: The forecastle on 17 August. A pile of teak planking, of unequal lengths, sits on the forecastle where some planking remains to be completed. The edge of the armoured belt has been marked off where a covering plate has been fitted. (NRS UCS1-118-418-102)

Below: The bridge and midships area giving a good overall idea of *Tiger*'s structural arrangements. Note work proceeding on the compass platform, the conning tower and rangefinder base and the interesting view into the 6in gun embrasure showing armoured and unarmoured sections of the structure. 17 August. (NRS UCS1-118-418-131)

Right: 25 August 1914. Working off pontoons, painters start on *Tiger*'s hull. The aftermost 6in gun is in place while, further forward, booms are being rigged. On the jetty at extreme right, a soldier with rifle stands guard. (NRS UCS1-118-418-112)

Left: 27 August. No 2 6in gun has now fitted as has the director on the spotting top. Several destroyers are under construction in the covered sheds in the background. (NRS UCS1-118-418-125)

Above: The remaining photographs show *Tiger* five weeks later when she is getting ready to leave Clydebank. Three members of her crew watch the photographer as he frames this view of *Tiger*'s freshly painted bow. Note the booms swung outboard. 2 October 1914. (NRS UCS1-118-418-134)

Right: What did not seem possible five weeks ago – *Tiger* now looking much more shipshape, painted, clutter removed and everything where it should be. Note the 3in gun on the shelter deck to the side of 'B' barbette and the two saluting guns on the deck above and behind that. 2 October 1914. (NRS UCS1-118-418-139)

Left: The quarterdeck showing various hatchways and skylights and last minute jobs being completed. Two workmen are removing the 'Keep clear of propellers' signs. Note the boom across the fitting-out basin, protection in the unlikely event that the yard was attacked from the River Clyde. (NRS UCS1-118-418-140)

Left: Another view taken on
2 October 1914.
(NRS UCS1-118-418-137)

Right: Close up of 'A' and 'B' turrets,
taken while the ship is being
provisioned. Crew members are starting
to outnumber shipyard workers.
(NRS UCS1-118-418-135)

Below: The starfish showing the spotting top with director tower above. The points of the starfish provide an anchor point for the various stays required to support the upper sections of the topmast. Also visible are footropes on the spars, Jacob's ladder at the rear of the topmast and signal and pendant halyards. The ship's siren, two of them, are fitted either side of the small platform immediately underneath the starfish. (NRS UCS1-118-418-139)

Above: A low angle shot of *Tiger*'s bridge, funnels and heavily rigged mast. Note what appears to be a lookout position at the junction of the topmast and topgallant and the ship's aerials and aerial spreaders.
(NRS UCS1-118-418-148)

Left: The ship does not yet have a full complement of boats. Note the main derrick, booms and funnel guys.
(NRS UCS1-118-418-143)

Above: A fine midships view of *Tiger* with boilers fired. The fall of light makes the turrets look paler than they are. (NRS UCS1-118-418-144)

Right: Another low angle shot of *Tiger*'s midships and the ever present 150-ton cantilever crane. The clouds of steam blowing off indicate that the safety valves on the boilers have lifted. (NRS UCS1-118-418-141)

Left: An excellent view of *Tiger*'s forward turrets and simple bridge structure. (NRS UCS1-118-418-145)

Left: 3 October 1914. The ship being provisioned via the gangway at the port bow prior to leaving the Clydebank yard to run trials.
(NRS UCS1–118–418–150)

Below: *Tiger* left Clydebank on 3 October to make the passage down the Clyde to the Tail of the Bank where she is seen here waiting for the pilot to board.
(NRS UCS1-118-418-163)

Right: A magnificent three-quarter bow shot of *Tiger* with the bow of the White Star liner *Olympic* in the background, 3 October 1914. After trials, *Tiger* sailed to Bantry Bay to continue gunnery and torpedo exercises arriving at Scapa Flow to join the 1st Battle Cruiser squadron on 6 November 1914.
(NRS UCS1-118-418-160)

SHIP No.443
REPULSE

The construction of *Repulse* began in circumstances that were wholly unusual and completely unlike the lengthy process-driven systems that brought *Inflexible*, *Australia* and *Tiger* into being. It was at the insistence of one man, Lord Fisher, that *Repulse* and her sister *Renown* were built at all. Fisher's return to the Admiralty as First Sea Lord in October 1914, two months after the outbreak of the First World War, brought with it his continuing passion for the battlecruiser type, the early war successes of which convinced him to push hard for two large, fast, heavily-armed but lightly-armoured ships, resulting in *Repulse* and *Renown*. Given that the most urgent need to complete the large warship building programme then underway was sufficient in itself to pressurise the shipbuilding industry, Fisher's intervention with two new ships to be built in record time was bold indeed. Average building times for the *Queen Elizabeth* and *Lion* class capital ships was in the region of thirty months not including the often lengthy design gestation period. At Fisher's insistence, the new battlecruisers were to be constructed in fifteen months with, in effect, no completed design to begin with, or, in the case of *Repulse*, no shipyard allocated for her construction. It would be a very cold start indeed. The building of both ships would test every aspect of the design, order and build (procurement) system then in place from Admiralty to shipyard with all of the numerous demands that would be made on the steel, armour and armament industries.

The Ship's Cover for *Repulse* and *Renown* includes an excellent précis of the origin of the contracts to build *Repulse* and *Renown*, written in August 1917. This précis, which communicates something of the urgency of the day, is quoted in part here:

> It was on the 19 December 1914 that the first intimation was given to the Director of Naval Construction that a new battle cruiser design was required: this ship was required to have a speed of 32 knots, with 6 – 15" guns, 2 pairs forward and one pair aft. The design was conceived as a direct result of the Falkland Islands battle and also on account of the experience gained during the actions fought on 28 August 1914, which showed the immense value of very high speed with long range powerful gunfire and large radius of action, which, in association, enable a ship to run down any of those of the enemy under any or all circumstances, with the power of accepting or declining action, as may be considered desirable. Features of such magnitude could only be obtained if the armour protection were comparatively light unless very great size of ships were accepted; the *Indefatigable* was taken as a standard type for protection with a 6" armour belt and 9" barbettes.
>
> On 21 December 1914, the dimensions of the new ship were arrived at and on the 24 December 1914, a model was made and inspected by Lord Fisher. Some modifications were asked for and incorporated and on 28 December the DNC was informed that the model was agreed to and that the design should be proceeded with.
>
> It was essential that the ships should be completed at the earliest

Right: The fine lines of *Repulse*'s bow, which was given more flare than her predecessors. The forward poppets are in place and the slipway is being prepared for launching. Although very few men are in this photograph, yard employment figures record almost 2700 men working on *Repulse* in December 1915. (NRS UCS1-118-443-156)

Opposite: *Repulse*'s stern partly obscured by a timber screen. Her rudder and shafts have been fitted although the propellers have not. The screen implies a heightened sense of secrecy during wartime, although the only difference between this battlecruiser and the preceding one is one large balanced rudder instead of two. Again the photographer is an irresistible attraction for workers. (NRS UCS1-118-443-129)

possible date, and at the suggestion of the DNC, the *Tiger's* machinery was, to all intents and purposes duplicated. A lighter design of machinery to develop the power required could have been obtained, but considerable time would have been spent in working it out, and the economy in time in adopting *Tiger's* machinery was very considerable, as patterns etc., were all available.

At this time, the *Repulse* and *Renown*, battleships of the *Royal Sovereign* Class, were in the early stages of construction at Messrs Palmers and Fairfield; the contracts for these ships were cancelled, and as Palmers were unable to build a vessel of the length required, 750 feet, John Brown & Co of Clydebank were given the order for the cruiser, *Repulse*, to replace the battleship of the same name. All the material ordered and delivered at Fairfields and Palmers for the battleships was looked into and as much as possible was used for the new ships, the material at Palmers being diverted to Clydebank.

On 29 December representatives of John Brown and Fairfield were interviewed by Lord Fisher and orders were placed for the new ships, the work to be carried out on a 'time and line' principle. It was laid down by Lord Fisher that the vessels should be completed in 15 months, but as seen later this abnormally short time was not realized.

By 17 January 1915, both firms were supplied with sufficient information to enable them to build the midship portion of the ship out to the turn of the bilge and to order much material, and the following drawings were supplied:

Complete body plan to lay off the vessel.
Position of bulkheads in machinery and magazine spaces.
Position of frames and longitudinals throughout double bottom.
Extent of double bottom.
Arrangement of spaces for oil fuel and reserve feed under machinery.
Modification to keel plates of battleship required to suit new vessel.
Table of thicknesses for outer bottom plates throughout ship up to waterline.
Outline particulars of stem and detail drawing of sternpost from which patterns for castings could be made.

On 25 January (Lord Fisher's birthday), the keels of both vessels were officially laid down. By 21 January the following information had been supplied to the firms:

Hull specification (first proof)
Complete midship section.
Part profile with figured dimensions for decks and flats.
Sections showing framing over the whole extent of double bottom.
Sections and figured dimensions for protective deck.
Sketch of extent of armour plating.
Sketch of armour giving rolling sizes for each plate.
Sketches of stem, sternpost, brackets and rudder.

This was sufficient to enable all the main structural and steel drawings to be prepared and the great bulk of the steel required for the hull to be ordered. By 15 February 1915, prints of the building drawings of the hold, platform and lower decks were sent to the firms, and by 28 February the building drawings of the main, upper and forecastle decks were completed.

By 12 April 1915, all the drawings, specifications and calculations usually made for a design were completed at the Admiralty, and on 22 April 1915, the design received the formal approval of the Board of the Admiralty.

In December 1914, the Clydebank yard had the following warships under construction – the battleship *Barham*, the cruiser *Canterbury*, the destroyers *Moorsom*, *Morris*, *Medea*, *Medusa*, *Marne* and *Mons*, and the submarine *E35*. Additionally, building berths were occupied by the P&O liner *Ormonde* and the small steamship *Stockholm* under construction for the Great Eastern Railway Co., later to become the seaplane carrier *Pegasus*. Conveniently, one large building berth, previously occupied by *Tiger*, was available in the East Yard and it was here that *Repulse* was laid down. Inserting such a large ship into an existing building programme and at such speed would have cut across all manner of procedures both in and outside the shipyard. *Repulse* was allocated the ship number 443 and number 3 berth was prepared in the East Yard. Shipyard management subsequently attempted to get the Admiralty to pay for lengthening the building berth and resulting adjustments to nearby buildings to accommodate *Repulse* but the Admiralty, who did underwrite the cost of structural work in shipyards, declined in this instance.

At the end of January 1915, the design was sufficiently advanced to allow orders for armour to be placed with most of the armour for *Repulse* going to John Brown's Atlas Works in Sheffield.

Side	1,120 tons
Bulkheads	130 tons
Barbettes	870 tons
Conning tower	65 tons
Total	2,185 tons

The delivery timetable specified bulkheads by the end of April, lower tiers of barbettes by the end of May, the remainder of 'Y' barbette by the end of July, the remainder of 'B' barbette by the end of August, the remainder of 'A' barbette by the end of September, the belt complete, excluding closers, by the end of September and finally, the conning tower by November. An approximate cost for the armour was given as barbettes £85,000 and belt £110,000.

Renown's armour contracts were split between Armstrong Whitworth, belt (starboard side), bulkheads, 'A' barbette and conning tower, (total 1,040 tons) and Cammell Laird, belt (port side), 'B' and 'Y' barbettes (total 1,145 tons).

The ship's principal castings were contracted as follows:

Stern casting A, The Steel Company of Scotland
Stern casting B, Wm Beardmore & Co.
Stern casting C, The Steel Company of Scotland and Thomas Firth & Sons
Stern and shaft tubes, Thomas Firth & Sons
Shaft tubes, Thomas Firth & Sons and F H Lloyd & Co.
Shaft brackets, Wm Beardmore & Co.
Rudder, Wm Beardmore & Co.

On 10 February, only eighty-two people were recorded as being employed on *Repulse* and of these, forty-four were iron workers most of whom would have been employed in the shops marking out, shearing and punching keel plates from templates supplied from the loft while most of the thirty-eight remaining were split between loftsmen and carpenters. Normally, labour was increased in step with the flow of information from the drawing office to the mould loft and finally the platers' shed. Given the speed with which this contract had moved from initial order to keel laying, the real effort initially would have been in the drawing office. With an understandable lag in the supply of information to the steel-working shops, serious efforts on the building berth although quick by normal standards were slow and could not maintain the momentum required by Fisher's timetable. In any case, labour shortages would have prevented a rapid start up. In January 1915, 4,943 men of all trades were employed in the shipyard, a number that had been reduced by 800 when *Tiger* left the yard in October 1914. Laying off and re-hiring large numbers of men like this was not uncommon despite future work in the pipeline as the yard could not pay men to do nothing before work materialised. Such were the vagaries of shipyard labour.

By 10 March, employment returns show that 341 men were working on *Repulse* of whom 248 were from the steel trades. Although John Brown management was doing all it could to speed progress, this was deemed to be insufficiently rapid. On 31 March, Lord Fisher, quick to express his concerns to the shipbuilder, went to the top and wired Lord Aberconway, Chairman of John Brown & Co:

I hear you have nothing like the number of men on *Repulse* that are required to complete her by the desired date. I had hoped that you would let nothing whatever prevent your pushing her on with the utmost speed possible. Please reply.

Aberconway replied the same day:

I regret exceedingly that progress hitherto made on the *Repulse* is not so good as we had hoped for. Our foremen have been doing everything in their power to obtain additional men accustomed to heavy type of ironwork during this past two months but the disappointing results of the efforts are entirely owing to the acceleration of mine sweepers and other Admiralty work in merchant shipyards and also to the Captain Superintendent of the Clyde's activity in having commandeered men to help in the acceleration of building of monitors on this river. I would venture to suggest that official instructions be issued to Captain Barttelot to commandeer for Clydebank Yard any men still available from the various merchant shipyards. With such official assistance in addition to our own efforts we would then hope to obtain the largely increased number of men required and thus to make quite a different showing from this time onwards and achieve her completion by the desired time.

If Fisher's wire had more than a hint of rebuke about it, Aberconway's response was illustrative of the wider problems facing the shipbuilding industry in the early months of the war, scarcity of labour and the priority attached to other naval work. The yard maintained high levels of production on the other urgently required warships in the yard, principally the cruiser *Canterbury*, four destroyers and two 'E' class submarines on the stocks as well as the battleship *Barham* and two destroyers fitting-out. Aberconway's reply neatly put the ball back in Fisher's court, suggesting that surplus labour such as there was in the Clydeside district, had been directed to urgent Admiralty work elsewhere on the river. The request that Captain Barttelot, the Naval Superintendent Clyde, assist in allocating labour to Clydebank had a fairly immediate effect. An inter-

view was arranged between yard management and Captain Barttelot at which it was agreed that by 6 April, forty platers (meaning fifteen platers and twenty-five helpers), thirty squads of riveters, forty caulkers and forty drillers would be found and sent to Clydebank.

By the end of April, employment in the yard stood at nearly 5,800 of whom 1,070 men from all trades were on *Repulse*, 851 of these being steelworkers. This enabled *Repulse* to be manned at a level more likely to give the shipbuilder a chance of meeting the delivery date.

Altogether, between January and May 1915, 1,400 men were added to the total payroll at Clydebank which then stood at 10,668 including the Engine Works. Numbers continued to rise slowly thereafter, peaking on 6 October when 1,949 ironworkers were recorded working on *Repulse*. The largest number of combined trades on this ship was on 22 December 1915, when a total of 2,841 men were employed exclusively on her.

Fisher maintained great interest in the new battlecruisers and despite resigning in May as First Sea Lord over the Gallipoli campaign, he visited Clydebank on Friday 18 June 1915 to see work in progress for himself. On this occasion, Thomas Bell commented that he 'appeared very much impressed with progress that has been made'.

Given the speed at which *Repulse* and *Renown* were to be built, it is hardly surprising to find that awkward decisions had to be made as the following memo from the DNC to the E-in-Chief, on 8 February, states: 'The conditions in connection with the above ships are such that it is necessary to omit everything not absolutely essential. From this point of view will you please state if you concur in the omission of the lifts to the turbine and condenser rooms observing that lifts to the boiler rooms are being provided for.' The E-in-C agreed with the omission of lifts to the engine rooms but insisted that lifts to condenser and boiler rooms be included.

The supply of main armament mountings, the major bottleneck where many capital ships were under construction also became an issue at the same time although mountings were in the contracts pipeline for the original battleships to be named *Renown* and *Repulse*. In this instance the issue was to get six mountings to the new battlecruisers as quickly as possible.

Work on 15" mountings of *Repulse* to be accelerated by all possible means but not to the prejudice of mountings already being accelerated.

Elswick asks if *Repulse* mountings are to take precedence over those for Royal Oak: if Royal Oak are required first, gun trials of *Repulse* not ready before March 1916 with delivery of mountings November and December. If *Repulse* takes precedence, gun trials in December 1915 with delivery of turrets September and October. Elswick [has been] informed that the following dates should be maintained and, if possible, anticipated:

Royal Oak	2 turrets by 2/10/15 gun trials 23/12/15
"	2 turrets by 30/10/15 " "
Repulse	2 turrets by 27/11/15 gun trials 20/2/16
"	2 turrets by 26/12/15 " "

Other issues concerned the speed at which the triple 4in secondary mountings could be delivered and a note from Fisher asks, most respectfully, if building them as breech-loading rather than semi-automatic would speed completion as breech-loaders were easier to make.

Modifications to the design, a natural sequence of events in more

Left: *Repulse* nearing the end of her launching run on 8 January 1916. The ship is well advanced for this stage with some of her belt armour and barbettes already in place. Note the bulges and deep bilge keels.
(NRS UCS1-118-443-175)

Left: This photograph taken shortly before the launch shows the arrangement of the shafts, shaft brackets and propellers as well as the poppet supporting the hull. The guy ropes crossing the image are used to hold the 5-ton derrick cranes in place, one of which can be seen at right.
(NRS UCS1-118-443-167)

Right: At rest in the water with her stern pointing towards the River Cart. The ship is flying the Union Jack, John Brown's house flag, an unidentified flag and the White Ensign.
(NRS UCS1-118-443-170)

leisurely times, had to be resisted. On 12 March 1915, both John Brown and Fairfield received a telephone call from the Admiralty concerning a proposal to increase the thickness of the longitudinal bulkheads 'Lord Fisher says if increase in thickness is going to cause delay they will resort to original thickness. Wire immediately [a] reply whether increase will cause delay.' Brown's wired later that day: 'Referring to your phone message this afternoon, we were originally of opinion that the delay in large cruiser due to introduction of heavy bulkhead would be at least two months and perhaps longer. Stop. After carefully considering the case again, we are confirmed in this conclusion. Stop.' The design of the bulkhead remained unchanged.

The monthly shipyard reports made by the shipyard describing progress of construction are missing for the War period. However, some indication of progress can be given through the reports filed by E L Attwood who visited both *Renown* and *Repulse* on a regular basis. Only a few of these reports have survived in the Ships' Covers.

Report from E L Attwood (constructor) to Berry (assistant DNC), 3 May 1915.

In accordance with your instructions, I visited the shipyards at Clydebank and Govan (on the 28, 29, 30 April and 1 May). In the yards there was a great advance since my last visit a month previously. At Clydebank, the ship was framed to the protective deck from submerged torpedo room to cut up aft, with most of the transverse and longitudinal bulkheads over this length. Two or three of the double bottom compartments had been surveyed, and were ready for water testing. The work of riveting the ship appeared to be progressing with a swing and it is understood that on the ship and in the shops about 1000 men are employed. Work on the thick main deck plating is in hand, from information supplied by the mould loft. All necessary information has been supplied by the drawing office well in advance of the requirements of the shipyard.

It is understood that work on the shaft brackets has been delayed owing to an accident at Messrs Beardmore's. A modification in the design of the long brackets by scarphing the arms is being made to facilitate casting of the same. It does not appear that the delay in the delivery of the castings will delay the progress of the ship... Each yard is making arrangements for sub-letting to small firms in the district, such work as they can do, to relieve pressure in the building yard, and the Overseers have requested the firms to extend this practice to the fullest possible extent.

Owing to the demand for copper, Messrs Brown are getting together information as to the possibility of the use of steel tubing for voice pipes and are obtaining samples of the tubes.

A model is being made in the Joiner's Shop, of Rig [and] Boat Stowage and I requested the firm to frost the glass of all the windows [in the shop] to keep the same from observation.

At Fairfield, *Renown* was off to a slower start and Attwood estimated she was one to two weeks behind *Repulse*.

In July 1915, shipyard and engineering works across the country were declared Controlled Establishments, in other words, they would now be organised in the national interest directly by the War Office. While a great deal of co-operation was already evident between shipyards and the Admiralty, this legislation gave the latter the ability to direct the flow of material and move labour as well as contracts from one yard to another. In September 1915, for example, the *Royal Sovereign* class battleship *Ramillies*, under construction at William Beardmore's Naval Construction Works at Dalmuir, was stripped of a number of iron workers, (platers and riveters) who were then redirected to *Renown* and *Repulse* to speed progress of construction. This was less damaging to the progress of *Ramillies* as she was in any case delayed for many months as her 15in main armament had been re-allocated to the monitors *Marshal Ney* and *Marshal Soult*, and the 'large light cruiser' *Glorious*.

At the progress conference held at Clydebank on 20 October 1915, Attwood, in his subsequent report, said that the Clydebank works manager, Thomas Bell, thought the ship would be launched at the end of January 1916. Hydraulic trials of the main armament could then take place in June which was about one month later than stated at the last conference. Bell pointed out that the firm had been instructed to cease Sunday working. 'If the firm could have a free hand in this matter and the weather was favourable, completion by the end of June could be promised with reasonable certainty. With no Sunday labour it will be the end of July and if the weather is bad it will be towards the end of August.'

By the time Attwood came to write his December report, the launch had been brought forward to 8 January 1916. With regard to the delivery of the 15in mountings, Attwood noted that priority might have to be given to mountings for monitors which would delay *Repulse* but on the other hand, by using two mountings from *Resolution*, there would be no delay and *Resolution* would not be affected. He noted that this matter was still under discussion with the Admiralty and gave the following report on *Repulse*:

The work on the *Repulse* is progressing very favourably. Boring out is completed and bushes etc., for propeller shafting are being put in place. Structure up to and including Forecastle Deck nearly all in position and being riveted off. Where decks have to be portable, butts and edges are bolted, with occasional rivets. All boilers on board and a considerable quantity of auxiliary machinery in engine rooms. Communication tubes in place and support to conning tower below forecastle deck in position. Steering gear now going on board. Rudder and crosshead in place. Hawse pipes in position. Work in store rooms started and electrical wires being run. Torpedo rooms, lip ends completed. All barbette armour in place. Weight at 14 December 1915 – steel 10,770 tons, armour about 1,150 tons. WTC (Water Tight Compartments) tested about 157.

At the time of this report, *Renown* was running about six to eight weeks behind *Repulse*. This was partly due to lack of labour and delays in providing her 15in mountings by the Coventry Ordnance Works.

Thomas Bell's report for December 1915 made reference to the actual construction period for *Repulse*, stating that: 'Thanks to excellent progress made on hull and also exceptionally quick delivery of huge propeller and stern tube shafts from our Atlas Works at Sheffield, the vessel will be ready for launch 9 months from actually commencing work on the building slip.' On 8 January 1916, *Repulse* was launched by the Duchess of Montrose at a weight of 15,156 tons. Thereafter the balance of work began to shift from the steel trades to the fitting-out trades. At the height of fitting-out in May 1915, a total of 2,168 men were employed on *Repulse* of whom 821 were from the steel trades. The first of *Repulse's* mountings arrived at Clydebank from Elswick on 28 April permitting a start to be made on the installation of the main armament. On 18 July 1916, orders, marked secret, were issued for *Repulse* to be commissioned at Clydebank on 8 August with a Chatham crew for service in the Grand Fleet (see Appendix 4, 'Manning levels on *Repulse*').

Repulse left Clydebank for the Tail of the Bank on 14 August and on the following day, the first of her steam trials took place on the newly-commissioned measured mile off the Isle of Arran on the Firth of Clyde. This course offered considerably deeper water than the Skelmorlie mile used hitherto and demonstrated that large ships running at high speed were faster in deep water. According to early reports from these trials, the 'depth effect' was equivalent to a loss of 3 knots in 20 fathoms and 6 knots in 12 fathoms over what could be expected in deep water. This was highly useful information given current operations in the shallow waters of the North Sea.

A four-hour full power trial was run at a displacement of 28,200 tons and a mean draught of 28ft 10.5in, She developed a mean of 117,000hp during the first two hours and a mean of 120,000hp over the second. On her last and fastest run she developed 125,350hp. *Repulse* returned to Clydebank for adjustments and then left the yard for the last time on 16 August. Gun trials took place on 18 August with satisfactory results. After docking at Portsmouth the ship made the passage north to join the fleet during which time she ran progressive steam trials on the Arran mile. On 15 September 1916, with a displacement of 29,900 tons, the ship was worked up over 4 hours 50 minutes from 12,450hp to 119,250 shp to give a speed of 31.725 knots. In the event, *Renown* would prove to be a little faster developing 126,300shp on her full power trial for 32.6 knots. *Repulse* was fully manned by naval personnel during the trials although the shipbuilder was asked to provide a small record party to take power and revolutions data (see Appendix 5, 'Record of Progressive Trials').

In his report for August 1916, Thomas Bell made one further comment about *Repulse*.

> While official time for construction from date of laying keel is 18.5 months it is only fair to say that the official date for laying the keel, 25 January 1915, was a paper date only to enable some official to wire Lord Fisher that it had been laid on his birthday. The designs were not sufficiently advanced nor was enough material in the yard to proceed with the work for another six weeks and even then it was with the greatest difficulty that working drawings could be prepared and approved to keep pace with the ship's construction.

The rapid construction of *Repulse* and *Renown* had demonstrated what could be achieved by the Admiralty and industry, particularly when the process was driven as hard as it was in the initial stages by Fisher. The précis referred to at the start of this section on *Repulse* concluded with regard to the speed of the ships:

> It is seen from the above, that the intentions of the design as regards speed were more than realized. The ship was delivered by the Contractors within about 19 months from the date of laying down. Having regard to the fact that the design was only in the outline stage when the ship was laid down, and that the ship was of a novel type, this performance is a remarkable one and constitutes a world record.

On 25 September 1916, their Lordships forwarded a letter to the DNC expressing and conveying to him and to the members of his staff

Above: This photograph taken on 15 December 1915 while the ship was still on the building slip shows the interior of 'Y' barbette. The ring bulkhead is visible on top of which is the lower part of the roller path (men are standing on this). The barbette armour is in place. (NRS UCS1-116-19-8)

concerned, 'their appreciation of the highly satisfactory and expeditious manner in which the work of designing, building and completing the Repulse, had been carried out'.

At the time that *Repulse* and *Renown* were in the last stages of completion, the inherent weaknesses of British battlecruisers after the battle of Jutland made them doubtful additions to the fleet. It was agreed that they should be fitted with additional protective plating at the earliest opportunity. The work involved the main and lower decks, armoured gratings, vertical bulkheads around the lower conning tower and the decks forming the crowns of the magazines. This work was to be undertaken at Rosyth Dockyard but the implications for other important work being carried out there meant that *Repulse* and *Renown* could not be taken in for some time. To obviate this, the Admiralty approached Clyde ship-builders John Brown, Wm Beardmore, Fairfield and Scotts, to ask if they could send men to Rosyth to carry out this work. John Brown and Fairfield agreed to this proposal and in the case of *Repulse*, John Brown replied that the work could be completed by December 1916. This addition to the original construction work for *Repulse* was referred to at Clydebank as Contract 443X. The work appears to have lasted from November 1916 to March 1917. John Brown's cost for this, principally labour, was a little in excess of £41,200.

No tender appears to have been submitted by the builder to the Admiralty at any time during construction. The only reference to *Repulse* in Clydebank's Tender Book was to note that the contract was to be treated in the following way:

> Hull: the percentage on wages for establishment charges will be 46%.
> Machinery: the percentage on wages for establishment charges will be 59%
> Profit will be 10% on the above.

The Comparison of Costs for *Repulse* provides the following figures:

Hull	£1,059,670 (presumably not including armour)
Machinery	£804,945

Right: 27 January 1916. *Repulse* is berthed at the east wharf of the fitting-out basin underneath the 150-ton derrick crane from which this photograph was taken. Deck plates have been bolted in place and will later be riveted and the bolts removed. The six box sections with a light covering of snow are watertight trunks that will be fitted vertically extending from the flying deck to a level below the shelter deck. Ahead of them, work is proceeding on the funnel casings. (NRS UCS1-118-443-188)

Left: This photograph taken on 12 April 1916 shows the gun shields of 'A' and 'B' turrets erected and the second 15in gun, weighing 100 tons, being lowered into position on its cradle in 'A' turret. The cruiser *Canterbury* and a destroyer are nearing completion in the background. (NRS UCS1-118-443-224)

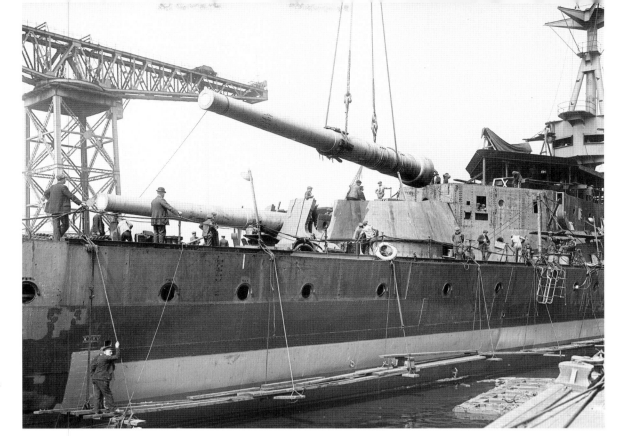

Right: 'Y' turret was the last of the three main armament turrets to be completed. In this photograph taken on 18 May, the second 15in gun is being lowered onto its cradle. (NRS UCS1-118-443-251)

Left: A good view of the midships area on 2 August with a 50ft pinnace and 32ft cutter in place. The blast screen for the triple 4in gun has been erected at the base of the mainmast although the mounting is still to be fitted in position beneath the 60ft main derrick. (NRS UCS1-118-443-290)

Above: *Repulse* essentially complete with the exception of her triple 4in mountings still to be fitted on the platforms to either side of the funnel. Note the extensive engine and boiler shops at the head of the fitting-out basin. (NRS UCS1-118-443-293)

Left: The flying deck is to the right of the mainmast with the torpedo control tower and the blast screen for the yet to be fitted 4in mounting. 'Y' turret has yet to be painted. Note the barrels waiting to be stowed and the diver's suit lying on the pontoon. (NRS UCS1-118-443-292)

Right: Another view of the ship's midship area taken on 2 August. Note the individual searchlight platforms at different heights on the two funnels. (NRS UCS1-118-443-293)

Above: In this view taken on 12 August, the triple 4in mountings on the flying deck and shelter deck are finally being fitted. Note the night lifebuoy at the deck edge. (NRS UCS1-118-443-301)

Left: A detail of the above showing battle honours on the night control tower with a 4in gun director above.

Left: *Repulse* at her berth with the 150-ton derrick crane that fitted her out. The ship with pennant number G83 is the 'R' class destroyer *Romola*, which was launched on 14 May 1916. (NRS UCS1-118-443-323)

Above: A view over the conning tower and forward turrets to the forecastle where part of the ship's crew, from Chatham, have been mustered. (NRS UCS1-118-443-295)

Opposite top: Three views of the triple 4in mountings that caused delays in the completion of *Repulse*.

Right: 12 August 1916. With two days left before she sails *Repulse* is a hive of activity. Her hull made extensive use of butt straps, which are visible in this shot. (NRS UCS1-118-443-300)

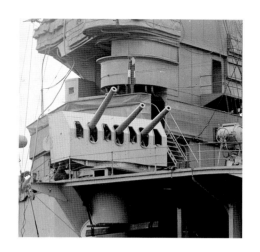

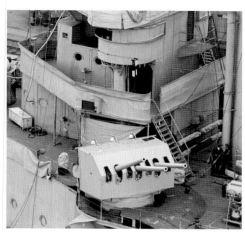

Above: To speed construction, the fitting of teak decks was omitted as this view over the forecastle shows. Note the cable holder, capstan and dark coloured blast bags on the 15in guns. *Romola* is in the background with two other 'R' class destroyers, possibly *Rowena* and *Restless*. (NRS UCS1-118-443-302)

Left: The ship from forecastle to bridge, 13 August 1916. (NRS UCS1–118–443–315)

Below: Detail of the conning tower and 15in director fitted with a 9ft rangefinder. Note the splinter mats and what appears to be a series of voice tubes fitted to the rear of the conning tower. (NRS UCS1–118–443–312)

Right: Note the White Ensign flying from the ensign staff (war position), the dark painted steel decks and the railway tank wagons presumably carrying oil fuel for *Repulse*. (NRS UCS1-118-443-316)

Above: Another excellent view of *Repulse*'s structural arrangements. (NRS UCS1-118-443-317)

Right: Details of the ship's boats neatly stowed on the forecastle deck to give the 4in triple on the shelter deck uninterrupted arcs across the ship.

Above: This low angle shot gives a better idea of the height that the 4in triple mounting on the conning tower platform is off the water.
(NRS UCS1-118-443-319)

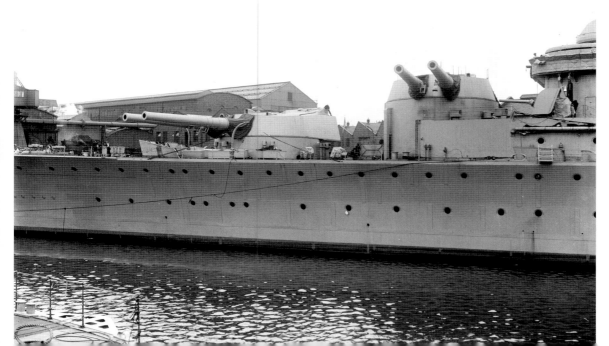

Left: The forward 15in Mk I guns in Mk I turrets.
(NRS UCS1-118-443-318)

Repulse: Ship No.443 • **117**

Left and Above: Two superb photographs of *Repulse* running trials on the Firth of Clyde, 14 August 1916. (NRS UCS1-118-443-4, & UCS1-118-443-330)

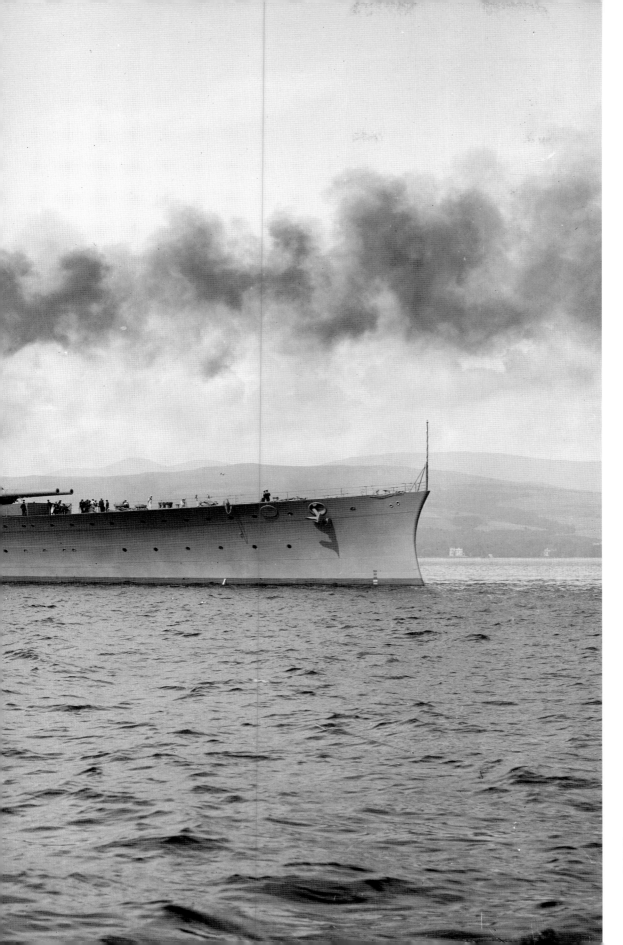

Left: The ship during trials on the Firth of Clyde, 14 August 1916. (NRS UCS1–118–443–327)

SHIP No.460
HOOD

In contrast to the four battlecruisers already discussed, *Hood*, a significantly larger ship, would take by far the longest time to build with nearly three-and-a-half years from keel laying to completion. This was partly because shipbuilding capacity was stretched to the limit. By 1916, there was no surplus pool of shipyard trades to attach to *Hood* without seriously affecting the progress of other important ships. The other reason for her delay was the consequences of the battle fought with the German High Seas Fleet at Jutland on 31 May 1916 which resulted in three British battlecruisers being sunk by German shellfire. The loss of three important ships with a high public profile and built at great cost to the nation was a cause for serious concern given that they were closely related in design and all lost in a similar manner. As the latest development of that design, *Hood* understandably came under much scrutiny by the Admiralty with serious delays in construction as her scheme of armour was re-worked.

The Board of the Admiralty issued instructions for the preparation of the design of a large battlecruiser on 8 March 1916 following lengthy discussions about armament, machinery, protection and various other aspects of design including the dry docks such large ships could be accommodated in. This stage of the design process as with previous ships, was characterised by memos circulated between department heads and the Sea Lords. Within a month, the design had been prepared and Board approval was given on 7 April for a ship with a displacement of 36,300 tons and a speed of 32 knots. Four ships were to be built and on 11 April, the First Lord met with the Chancellor of the Exchequer to approve the new programme of shipbuilding including four battlecruisers. Under the terms of the Munitions of War Act 1915, the Admiralty had control of the shipbuilding industry and thus knew where the orders for these ships would be placed without the need for tendering. The great length of the new ships in any case precluded many shipyards on the Admiralty list and only the yards with the longest slips were in contention. One each of the new ships went to John Brown, Cammell Laird and Fairfield. A fourth, intended to be placed with Armstrong Whitworth, was delayed for three months pending the outcome of discussions concerning the Chilean battleship *Almirante Cochrane*. The terms of business were simple and straightforward; orders were placed on a fixed contract price and the firms asked to quote their price as soon as possible. The shipyards were told they could start work immediately on condition that they agreed to 'accept the decision of the Admiralty', meaning that the latter would be able to have the final say on prices submitted by the shipbuilder.

A letter formally placing the contract was sent to each of the three yards on 19 April. Importantly, this letter set out the level of priority to be attached to the pace of construction. Work should proceed at first only at such a rate as will employ a nucleus of men accustomed to heavy frame work, involving the least call on labour and material required by them for the war vessels being rapidly completed for the war and for merchant ships urgently required for carrying cargo. If you accept this order, information as regarding details of machinery and boilers would be supplied at once to your representative at the Admiralty and sufficient information would be furnished to you within about 10 days from now to enable them to proceed with the framework of the lower part of the ship.

In the same month, based on basic information about the ship provided by the DNC, namely, eight 15in in four turrets, sixteen 5.5in, two 21in torpedo tubes (not decided upon), 144,000shp and complement as flagship, her complement was worked out and thus the ship's accommodation requirements determined.

In the usual manner, drawing office workload was shared between the respective shipbuilders initially John Brown, Fairfield and Cammell Laird. When Armstrong Whitworth were subsequently given the order for *Anson*, work was further subdivided to include them.

The only minuted comment about the new battlecruiser so far recorded at Clydebank was on 3 May 1916 when it was stated that the firm had been notified by the Admiralty to prepare for a ship similar to *Repulse*.

On 31 May 1916, the battle of Jutland was fought with significant consequences for the design of *Hood* given the catastrophic loss of three battlecruisers and 3,311 men. The immediate seriousness of this tragic outcome can well be imagined within the Admiralty as steps were taken to understand what had caused the loss of these ships and their crews and ensure that the design of the new battlecruisers was reassessed as a consequence. The following sequence of memos gives some idea of the events that took place at the Admiralty and on board the ships of the Grand Fleet in Scapa Flow.

18 June 1916 from Rear Admiral Pakenham [writing from the battlecruiser *Australia*] to Vice Admiral Beatty Commanding the Battle Cruiser Fleet.

New Construction

Sir,
After consulting with [the] Director of Naval Construction, who acquainted them [the Committee] with the general nature of the present proposals of the Admiralty for constructing armoured

Above: *Hood's* keel and double bottom plating looking forward to the head of the building berth in September 1916. (Author's collection)

vessels of great size and speed, the Committee appointed by your Memorandum BCF 29, are of opinion that in those vessels above water protection is quite inadequate for action even with existing vessels, and therefore, however great their other qualities, they would be in a position of still greater inferiority relative to the future construction that our enemy may confidently be expected to undertake.

Your Committee therefore desire to submit as a matter of urgency that the Admiralty be requested to arrange further meetings between Admiralty representatives and your Committee while designs are still capable of modification.

Signed by members of the Committee. [Names given]

On the same day Beatty replied:

I entirely concur as to the desirability of further meetings between representatives of the Admiralty Constructive Department and Officers who have had the experience of action conditions. Such an

'ADMIRAL' CLASS: DIVISION OF DRAWING OFFICE WORK

J Brown	Fairfield	Cammell Laird
After framing elevation	Forward framing elevation	Deck coverings
After framing sections	Forward framing sections	Protective decks
Castings, sternpost & rudder	Castings, stem	Upper, forecastle shelter & other deck plating
Shaft brackets	Keel, vertical & flat plates	Screen & shelter bulkheads
Beam arm & frame fastenings	Longitudinals	Boiler bearers
Transverse bulkheads	Scheme of riveting bulkheads	Plating behind armour
Flats, aft	Flats, forward	Pillaring arrangements
Barbettes, framing & plating (including supports to barbettes)	Body plan & trace of longitudinals	Cabin & minor bulkheads
Engine seatings (above & below lower deck)	Expansion OB plating	Water testing (scheme of)
Auxiliary engine seats	Expansion of IB plating	Anchor & cable arrangements★
Shaft tube framing (including framing & plating behind armour belt)	Longitudinal & wing bulkheads	Shipping engine & boiler & aux machinery arrangements
Gunnery & torpedo arrangements★	Armour arrangements & details of plates including barbettes	Bridges★
Magazine & shell rooms★	Funnel & ventilation casings★	Mast, struts, derrick post & derrick★
Steering gear	Framing expansion	Rig★
Oil fuel arrangement	Armour gratings	Ladderways, skylights including key plan of hatches
Weather deck fittings	Escape trunks & sliding shutters	Workshops
Boat stowage	Conning & torpedo control towers with communication tubes★	Galleys
Messing, sleeping & cabin arrangts.	Fan flats & casings	Bakery, kitchens etc.
Ventilation arrangements including magazine cooling arrangements	Pumping, flooding & draining arran.	Store rooms
Sick bay	Fresh & salt water agmts including WCs, bath rooms urinals & seamen's WCs ★	Lagging & lining of cabins
Turbine & lifting gear & traversing arrangements	Voice-pipe agmts including telephone both systems	Offices
Electric light & power arrangements	WT doors and manholes including OT manholes	Painting scheme
Ring main & control cables	–	1/16" scale plans

★ denotes work later given to Armstrong Whitworth's drawing office once their contract had been placed.

opportunity of obtaining first hand information has never occurred before, and I must submit that the greatest possible use should be made of it at the earliest possible moment.

On 22 June 1916 Admiral Jellicoe aboard *Iron Duke* noted that '… be pleased to inform the Lords Commissioners of the Admiralty that I consider it very desirable that the opinions of Naval Officers who have been in action afloat should be sought on this matter, due regard being paid to the undesirability of seriously delaying the completion of ships'.

On the same day the DNC, Sir Eustace d'Eyncourt wrote to the Third Sea Lord, Frederick Tudor:

After inspecting damaged ships at Rosyth on 15 inst., I attended a conference on board HMS Australia, RA Pakenham presiding. We discussed the question of adding to the protection of various ships, and of arrangements for stopping flash to magazines. At the request of RA, I explained briefly some of the features of the New Battle Cruiser design. The information I gave, was not, however, in my opinion, sufficient to enable the officers present, to form a sound judgement of the qualities of the design as a whole: and they had not considered the question of underwater protection at all.

I quite concur with the view expressed by the VA BCF [Beatty] that conferences between officers who have had experience in action and constructive officers are very advisable, and personally I learnt a great deal at the discussions I had with officers of the Grand Fleet and also of BC Fleet.

The following day the Third Sea Lord commented:

Immediately after the action, officers of the DNC's department were dispatched to examine and report on damaged ships, and later, DNC visited all the fleets involved and has reported. The designs of the new battlecruisers are being carefully scrutinised by his department with a view to expressing possible improvement, as the result of recent experiences.

As regards the communication from the Vice Admiral, Battle Cruiser Fleet, I suggest that it be referred to C-in-C., stating that whilst concurring that consultations between DNC or officers of his department with officers of the Fleet, in connection with modifications of design and repairs are useful, as regards new designs, Their Lordships are always prepared to receive proposals and suggestions based on actual experience from officers serving in the Fleet which would be duly considered in conjunction with other requirements.

While the above events resulted in a significant recast of the armour scheme which would emerge many months later, construction of the ship at Clydebank continued at low priority while the order for the fourth ship of the class was placed with Armstrong Whitworth on 13 June. With no engine building capacity, Armstrong later subcontracted the machinery for their ship to Hawthorn Leslie. However, on the same day, the Admiralty wrote to John Brown to inform them that the low priority given to No 460 had been removed and that their ship 'should be fully proceeded with under ordinary conditions, no special steps being taken however to work under accelerated conditions'. This increase in priority applied to Clydebank's ship only, the other three

remaining at a low priority. The Minutes at Clydebank for June simply note that they had received a letter from the Admiralty saying that the Treasury had agreed that one of the new battlecruisers was to proceed. 'It is to be ours, No 460.' The reason why John Brown's ship was chosen over the others, two of which were not significantly behind at this stage, is not clear.

Labour returns made weekly at Clydebank show that by the third week in June, a total of forty-eight men were working on No 460 including twenty-eight ironworkers, five loftsmen and five carpenters. This indicates that the ship's lines were laid or being laid off in the mould loft and that the first of the steel plates that would form her keel were in preparation in the Plater's Shed.

The main hull castings for the ship were placed with:

Stem, Thomas Firth & Sons.
Shaft tubes, Thomas Firth & Sons.
Shaft brackets, stern frame, stern frame portion C, propeller bracket, rudder frame, all Wm Beardmore & Co.

With the reconsideration of the design likely to affect armour protection and not the main armament, at the end of June (the 26th), the Admiralty placed provisional orders for the 15in main armament (a new Mark II design with 30° elevation) for all four ships of the class as follows:

Company	Sets	Condition
Vickers	1 (4 turrets)	Peace condition *(Hood)*
Vickers	1	Slow condition
Armstrong	1	Slow condition
Coventry Ordnance Works	1	Slow condition

Peace conditions, a faster rate of construction than slow condition, matched the increased rate of construction that would be applied to the John Brown ship over her three sisters.

By 5 July 1916, the DNC had produced the first of a series of proposed modifications to the protection of the new battlecruisers.

In accordance with instructions given me by 3SL [Third Sea Lord] at the conference held on 26 June, the attached drawings, 2 in number, showing proposed modifications to the armour and deck protection of New Battle Cruiser are submitted herewith for approval.

Attention is drawn to the following points, viz;-

320lb. armour belt increased in depth by 1' 8"
200lb. armour below Upper Deck reduced to 120lbs.
Lower Protective Deck increased from 60lbs. to 80lbs.
Barbette armour between decks increased in thickness.
Space round 5.5-inch ammunition hatches and dredger hoists on Main Deck enclosed by 40lb. bulkhead.

The net effect of these alterations is an increase in weight of about 500 tons or about 4 inches of draught. The 4 additional dynamos approved and the new torpedo arrangements now under consideration will probably involve another 2 inches of draught, or altogether about 6 inches, which will involve a slight reduction of speed, say 1/8th of a knot.

Left: Forward section of the double bottom showing the basic arrangement of plates with lightening holes and longitudinals – all riveted together with angle iron. Each plate is numbered and carries numerous other instructions. (Author's collection)

Opposite, centre: The hand-drawn 'stamp' applied to Board of Admiralty minutes.

Right: The forward section showing plating of the inner bottom underway and frames towards the bow erected. (Author's collection)

Legend draft (mean) will become 26 feet and deep draught 29.5 feet. If turret roof plates are made 200lbs. instead of 170, there will be a further increase of 45 tons, and if front plates are made 600lbs (15-in) it will add 16 tons more.

On 11 July the Third Sea Lord noted with regard to the above.

I am very anxious to improve the protection on the turrets, the weak points being the roof plates and front plates. The 170lb. Vanadium plate of 'Malaya' has proved satisfactory against a heavy projectile, but is very near the limit and I consider the new ships should have not less than 200lb. roofs of the new quality vanadium steel or its equivalent, and 15-inch front plates. I have discussed this with DNC and he concurs.

I believe the disposition of armour now proposed for these new battle cruisers to be as good as can be devised for the protection of the vitals, without adding still more weight, but it must be remembered that these vessels were intended to be very fast, fairly shallow draught, torpedo proof battle cruisers, and the more general protection given them, the more they will depart from this conception. With the amount of armour now proposed and the invariable additions which experience shows they will be subject during construction, their speed under war conditions will probably lie between 30 and 31 knots and their draft will approximate to that of some of our older battleships. Propose to approve as submitted.

From the Grand Fleet, Jellicoe (16 July) also thought the roof plates should be 6in thick although the Director of Naval Ordnance pointed out that the roof plates for *Hood* had already been rolled at 5in thick. He said they could be temporarily fitted while the other three ships of the class could have 6in from the start.

On 14 July 1916, the Ship Branch announced that the new ships were to be named after Admirals *Anson* (Armstrong), *Hood* (Brown), *Howe* (Cammell Laird) and *Rodney* (Fairfield).

Throughout the months that followed, a series of new proposals were put forward by the DNC to the Board for approval. In addition to a heavily revised scheme of armour, the bridges and torpedo control and rangefinder positions were altered all of which ensured that a final set of building drawings could not be prepared. This did not prevent work on *Hood* proceeding slowly at Clydebank however, as the portions of the hull that would be built first were unaffected. With sufficient material now prepared in the shops the keels of all four ships were laid within nine weeks of one another.

Hood	(Ship No 460)	1 September
Rodney	(Ship No 527)	9 October
Howe	(Ship No 834)	16 October
Anson	(Ship No 909)	9 November

At the beginning of November, the managers meeting at Clydebank noted that 'sufficient information is gradually being obtained from the Admiralty to enable more material to be ordered for this vessel and to employ a few more men on her construction, but in view of the alterations in her design, comparatively slow progress can only be made until the beginning of next year'.

By the time her keel was laid on 1 September, 150 men were working on the ship. By the beginning of November this number had risen to 300. At the Admiralty, however, what would prove to be a lengthy series of alterations and enhancements to the protection of the battlecruisers had begun. This suited the slow pace of construction as otherwise areas of her structure were as yet undecided. The original design for a ship of 36,300 tons and 32 knots had been approved by the Board on 7 April 1916. As a result of Jutland, the DNC's revised design for a ship of 40,600 tons was approved on 13 September 1916 while a re-arrangement of this armour scheme was approved on 2 October. This scheme was referred to the C-in-C Grand Fleet, and the modifications made as a result were approved on 14 December 1916. However it was not until 20 August 1917 that the design was finalised in all its detail and only then could the sheer drawing, and drawings of the midship section be completed.

'… with all dispatch'
On 10 February 1917, the Secretary of the Admiralty sent the following telegram to the Captain Superintendent, Clyde District, Brian Barttelot.

[The] Following telegram has been sent today to John Brown & Co. (begins) 'Admiralty has decided that work on Hood is to be completed with all dispatch. Please arrange accordingly communicating with captain Superintendent Clyde district and overseers.' (Ends) You are to hold a conference with contractors at which the overseers and representatives of Admiralty Departments are to attend to consider best means of giving effect to this decision with least interference to merchant shipbuilding and with other Admiralty work. Antisubmarine construction must under no circumstances be affected. Report should be forwarded as soon as possible which should state earliest date by which completion of vessel can be relied upon.

This telegram was copied to the overseers at Clydebank, E D Meryon, Hull Overseer, and Eng Cdr L J Stephens, Machinery Overseer, and the conference duly held at Clydebank. At the end of the conference, Barttelot forwarded the following status report to the Secretary of the Admiralty:

Hull
Messrs J Brown request that:-

The general working drawings of the pumping system and flooding arrangements throughout the ship be approved by the end of February.

That the general electrical specification and also the specification of the generating machinery be received by the end of February. Very great importance is attached to the receipt of these specifications, as the progress of the ship is dependent thereon.

A definite decision as to the design and position of the structural components to the Conning Tower may be communicated by the end of February.

Definite decisions be given on the oil fuel filling heating and suction arrangements by the end of February.

The iron work being in advance of the work on the various fittings connected with the pumping, flooding, oil fuel filling and heating arrangements, it will not be necessary for increased delivery of steel structural material to be made for the next 6 or 7 weeks; but subsequent to that date, delivery of further steel material at the rate of 2,500 to 3,000 tons per month will be required during May, June, July and August.

Machinery

The firm ask for priority to be given:-
a) To the whole of the steel forgings for the turbines, gear wheels and propeller shafting.
For iron castings obtained in this district.
For the solid drawn steel piping and flanges required for the oil fuel heating and other connections.
For the copper tubing, brass fittings and for the drawn steam piping.

Armament

The firm request that:-
'A' and 'B' turrets be delivered end of May 1918.
'X' and 'Y' turrets be delivered end of July 1918.

Sunday Work

Messrs John Brown lay great stress on their request to be allowed to work certain sections of their men on Sundays whenever they consider it necessary to facilitate certain work.

Labour

The hull is considerably ahead of the oil fuel and pumping connections, acceleration during March and April must be confined to the latter nature of work: consequently no increase in the number of ironworkers will be necessary until May or June. It is hoped that the Firm's demands will then be small, as it is difficult to see where men will be obtained from without prejudicing mercantile shipbuilding.

Date of Completion

Messrs John Brown undertake, provided the various requests embodied in this report are complied with, to complete the ship ready for trials by November 1918.

While the Admiralty did what it could to supply the shipbuilder with the information requested, there was little it could do with the supply of the main armament under construction at Vickers which would be the cause of significant delay in completing the ship. The Admiralty also chose to disagree with the shipbuilder's request to employ Sunday labour, an unfortunate consequence of being a 'Controlled Establishment' as shipyard management saw it. The Admiralty's view, a rather selective one, was centred on the well-being of management as this sentence from their letter to John Brown states – 'no provision can be made to relieve the great strain upon the health of the directing staffs and the ultimate adverse effect upon output'.

By late February 1917, the scheme of protection for *Hood* had been sufficiently developed to permit a series of contracts for the supply of armour to be placed. Consequently, on the 24th of that month the Director of Naval Contracts placed orders in the following way:

Company	Armour
John Brown	480lb (12in) belt armour lower tier starboard side. 1,130 tons.
Vickers	Upper tiers of barbettes. Lower tier barbette armour and armoured bulkheads had been ordered on 13 December 1916.
Cammell Laird	480lb lower tier belt armour port side. 1,130 tons.
Beardmore	Middle and upper tiers of belt armour starboard side and belt forward and aft of the main belt. Total 946 tons.
Armstrong	Middle and upper tiers of belt armour port side and belt forward and aft of the main belt. Total 946 tons.

As was the case with all armour, the plates had to fit accurately against the structure of the hull and with one another. This necessitated making wooden templates taken directly off the hull which were sent to the steel works where the plates were to be made. In recognition of this effort and the distribution of armour to each of the large UK armour mills, the Admiralty explained to management at Clydebank that:

It is hoped by this arrangement not only to give the several armour plate makers a reasonable share of the armour, but also to secure it in ample time to meet the needs of the ship. The Admiralty recognize that this arrangement will involve a greater demand upon Clydebank shipyard for moulds etc., than would otherwise be the case, but the Admiralty have invited the cordial co-operation of the several armour plate makers to secure good fit etc., and they rely upon the shipyard branch of your firm taking in conjunction with the armour firms all necessary steps, and supplying all necessary moulds and information to ensure the best possible result.

In the letter of contract to John Brown and Cammell Laird from the Admiralty regarding the belt armour above, it was noted that:

as you have not produced a sample plate to meet the new specification attack by 13.5" projectiles they [the Admiralty] are prepared, to avoid delay, to accept armour as per their 480lb sample provided it meets the ballistic requirements of 12" attack. It is hoped however that you will shortly succeed in producing a satisfactory sample plate under 13.5" attack in order that as much as possible of that armour may be manufactured on that basis.

It would be surprising to think that the Admiralty would have allowed the inferior plates to be fitted as this letter implies.

With the main armour contracts placed, the Admiralty turned to important but smaller contracts:

Company	Armour
Hadfields	Forward communications tube 3in thick and 33in internal diameter.
Beardmore	After communications tube 4in thick and 30in internal diameter.

At the same time, Bow McLachlan & Co Ltd., of the Thistle Works, Paisley, were contracted to provide the steering gear.

Early in March 1917, the DNO expressed the desirability of reversing the position of the shell and magazine rooms for 'A' and 'B' turrets as well as for the forward 5.5in guns. He also asked that the 15in transmitting station and lower conning tower should be repositioned under the water-line. The DNC replied on 21 March that the forward part of *Hood* was already in course of erection and that to reverse the shell and magazine rooms on 'A' and 'B' turrets would retard progress on the ship. It was still possible, however, to make this change to the 5.5in guns. He recommended not making the change to 'A' and 'B' turrets on *Hood* but that it should be applied to the other three ships of the class. Drawings of the 5.5in arrangements were sent to John Brown soon after.

In spite of this development and potential cause of further delay, the C-in-C Grand Fleet was pushing hard for the ship prompting the Third Sea Lord, Frederick Tudor, to write to all departments on 17 March:

> In view of the fact that Hood is to be completed as quickly as possible, steps should be taken by the departments to ensure that full information is furnished to the contractors so as to enable work to proceed at full dispatch: it is also most necessary that no alterations in the gunnery, torpedo, electric etc. fittings should be introduced in this ship with consequent risk of delay.

Although the three sister-ships had been suspended in March, the following month, orders were placed for their auxiliary machinery with Cammell Laird for *Howe*, to Fairfield for *Rodney* and to Hawthorn Leslie for *Anson*.

In early June, further orders for *Hood* were placed with Smith Major & Stevens Ltd, Abbey Works, Northampton, for sixteen electric lifts at a price of £7,100; Napier Bros, Hyde Park Street, Glasgow, for the forward capstan; Burfield & Co, Blaydon Iron Works, Newcastle upon Tyne, for the after capstan. Later that month, the Admiralty advised John Brown to accept Thomas Firth & Sons, Sheffield, tender for the 15in control tower for *Hood* and to decline the tenders from Hadfields and Armstrongs.

Meanwhile, deliberations on the thickness of the turret roof plates were still in progress prompting Admiral Beatty, C-in-C Grand Fleet, to write to the Secretary of the Admiralty on 6 June stating that he thinks it is essential that the roof plates of the Hood Class should be 6in vana-dium steel. 'If it is found impossible to fit the heavier plates in the "HOOD" owing to her advanced construction, it is submitted that plates of a minimum thickness of six inches of vanadium steel may be fitted in the other vessels of the class.' Discussion on this subject ensued between the DNO and DNC until mid July although it was noted that new plates of 200lb and 240lb were about to be tested but that the plates for *Hood* had already been rolled and treated.

At the end of August, the design of the after part of the ship was sufficiently advanced to permit the ordering of armour for the after torpedo control tower from John Brown's Sheffield Works. The walls of the tower were to be made from four 240lb plates keyed together, the slot to be machined out of the solid. The 160lb roof plate was specified to be turret roof quality.

By September 1917, the question of pushing work forward on the three other ships of the Class came to a head when it was realised that making significant progress on these ships would paralyse production elsewhere. The Third Sea Lord (Lionel Halsey), considered that no action could be taken to hasten the construction of the three battlecruisers and proposed that the only alternative was 'that most energetic action be taken to induce the Japanese to help us by letting us have some of the Kongo Class'. A decision on the three suspended ships was awaited from the First Sea Lord, John Jellicoe. On 15 October he wrote:

> In regard to the question of battlecruiser construction and expediting the completion of HOOD, the Naval Staff is unable to suggest any items in the shipbuilding programme which could be sacrificed for this purpose, unless it is possible to suspend work on the light cruisers RALEIGH and EFFINGHAM and to transfer the labour and men to the HOOD. The Commander-in-Chief, Grand Fleet, who discussed this matter with the Deputy First Sea Lord, expressed the view that the completion of the HOOD should be expedited, whatever the sacrifice.

By an interesting quirk of fate, Thomas Bell, shipyard director at Clydebank, had been appointed as Deputy Controller of Dockyards and War Shipbuilding in May 1917, and thus became involved in the labour issues surrounding *Hood* and her sister-ships. His report to the Controller on 4 October 1917, describes how acute the shortage of labour had become. One suggestion, briefly considered, was to recruit miners into the shipbuilding industry, presumably as labourers. This proposition was seriously considered in a meeting on 28 September between the Controller and the Minister for National Service, Auckland Geddes. It was recognised however, that this would result in miners, wanting to retain their existing wage levels, and thus being paid more than an expert plater's helper or even platers themselves, 'resulting in serious demands for wage increases by the whole of the ironworkers in existing shipyards with consequent unrest and loss of production all over the Country'. Bell's report continued by pointing out that acceleration of *Hood* was only possible at the expense of other shipbuilding.

> If it is decided that the position of HOOD was the same as that of steel and other raw materials, acceleration is only possible at the expense of other shipbuilding. If it be decided that acceleration of the HOOD is of prime necessity, the preferable way of effecting this would be to delay the construction of the oilers, standard ships and destroyers building in the same yard and thereby confine the disturbance of shipbuilding production to one yard.

Bell pointed out that both the DNC and DNO considered that *Hood* could be completed by December 1918 provided an early decision is made to accelerate her construction.

In an effort to do this, the shipbuilder pointed out that one month could be saved on completion if the crushing tubes were omitted from the after and fore end of the ship, abreast the magazines. Because of the fine lines of the ship, the complex shape of these bulge compartments made stowing the crushing tubes a time-consuming activity. The DNC replied that if the bulges were not fitted with tubes, it would be necessary to increase flooding arrangements to compensate for the loss of buoyancy. The work involved thereby would have no effect on speeding her construction.

The decision was delivered on 25 October 1917 when the Board of the Admiralty decided that it was not advisable to accelerate *Hood* given the effect this would have on the shipbuilding programme. This decision must have caused Beatty great concern given the depleted nature of the battlecruiser force against expected future German battlecruiser strength.

Labour records at Clydebank show that in September, 1,541 men were working on the ship a figure that rose to 1,687 at the beginning of October. This was about 1,000 men short of what would have been required to complete the ship by the end of 1918. As labour became available from completed contracts elsewhere, manning on *Hood* continued to rise slowly month by month and did not reach its peak until July 1918 when 2,679 men were employed solely on this ship.

At the end of December 1917, John Brown & Co felt they had a sufficient idea of the ship they were building to put forward the following estimated cost of the ship:

Hull

Structural materials	532,000	
Outfit materials	212,500	
Dredging, light, coal etc. less scrap	63,000	808,000
Wages		800,000
Charges at 38 per cent		304,000
		1,912,000

Machinery

Materials engines	522,000	
Materials boilers	92,000	614,000
Wages engines	175,000	
Wages boilers	66,000	241,000
Charges at 50 per cent		120,500
		975,500

Hull		1,912,000
Machinery		975,500
		2,887,500
Auxiliaries	72,500	
		2,960,000
Profit	288,750	
Total		**3,248,750**

On 26 March 1918, a conference held at Clydebank endeavoured to assess progress and give a date for completion of the ship given that she had not, after all, been accelerated. The level of importance attached to this meeting can be measured by those in attendance: Admiral Green, Senior Naval Officer Clyde; Admiral Phillpotts, Director of Naval Equipment, with representatives of the Gunnery and Torpedo Departments; W J Berry, Director of Warship Production; E L Attwood, representing the DNC; C H Wordingham, Director of Electrical Engineering; H J Blandford, Warship Production Superintendent; Hull, Machinery, Gun Mounting and Electrical Overseers; Mr Thackary and Mr Chapman, of Vickers Ltd, Gunnery Contractors and finally, representatives of John Brown & Co, the shipbuilders.

The basic findings of the conference were that the ship could be ready for launching in August or September 1918. The construction of the barbettes would be sufficiently advanced to allow Vickers access to install the turntables etc., by the end of August for 'A' turret, the end of September for 'B' turret and the end of October for 'X' and 'Y' turrets, assuming the ship had been launched. If the heavy weights of 'X' and 'Y' turrets were installed by the end of November, the propelling machinery, shafting etc, could then be properly aligned and completed. It was noted

that work on the transmitting station at the base of the conning tower and director work in the tower was of 'great magnitude and complexity'. If all of the above could be completed, the ship could be ready by May 1919. However, the Vickers representative could offer no guarantees that the dates for the supply of the gun mechanisms could be met in their entirety. For John Brown, the shipyard and engine works managers said they were making very rapid visual progress with the ship, and, in regard to the 'frequent difficulties and delays in obtaining materials and items of outfit from sub-contractors, a decision on all outstanding points was required forthwith and delivery of all items to be supplied would be continually urged by them'. From this it would seem that the main cause of delay in completing the ship would be Vickers, unable to give a date for delivery of her main armament.

The Ships Cover contains an undated statement which fits with the above report but is written with a degree of overview and reflection perhaps intended for a wider audience:

The alteration in the design of Hood when her armour and protection were considerably increased took place at a very early stage in her construction and did not of itself involve any longer period for construction. It was decided not to 'accelerate' the ship and the work was for some time given a low order of priority as compared to other work at Clydebank.

The reinforcement of the magazine crowns recently decided upon will hardly affect the final date of completion, in view of the late delivery of the gun mountings, which is the determining feature. If the gun mountings were delivered to suit the progress of the ship, it is probable that the ship could be delivered in May or June 1919, but at the recent conference, John Brown's declined to give even an approximate date for delivery.

In early April, it was approved to add lagging to the bulkheads and the crowns of the magazines at an additional weight of 45 tons. Soon after this however, a memo was circulated around the relevant departments at the Admiralty that in order to prevent further delay no additional alterations were to be made without Board approval.

Meanwhile, decisions were pending on the three other ships of the class on which little or no progress had been made. In April 1918, the War Cabinet decided that under the shipbuilding programme for 1919, work on *Howe* should proceed but that work on *Anson* should be deferred. This was ratified on 15 May when the Naval Expenditure, Emergency Standing Committee stated that the Lords Commissioners of HM Treasury were pleased to sanction 'the continuation of work on HMS Howe, one of the three battle cruisers for which £10m was sanctioned by the Treasury in 1 April 1916, instead of on HMS Anson'. There was no mention of *Rodney* at this stage. However, the Admiralty was pressing for two of the battlecruisers to be resumed at the normal rate and at a meeting of the War Cabinet on 4 September, the decision was made to defer the decision until the end of the year. In December, the Fairfield yard was advised by the Admiralty that 'as regards Rodney it should be assumed, in making the future programme for the work in your yard, that this vessel will remain as at present, i.e. no expenditure for labour or material is to be incurred on her'.

Hood was launched by Lady Hood on 22 August with a displacement of 21,720 tons and a mean draught of 15ft 6in. At this stage her condition was as follows:

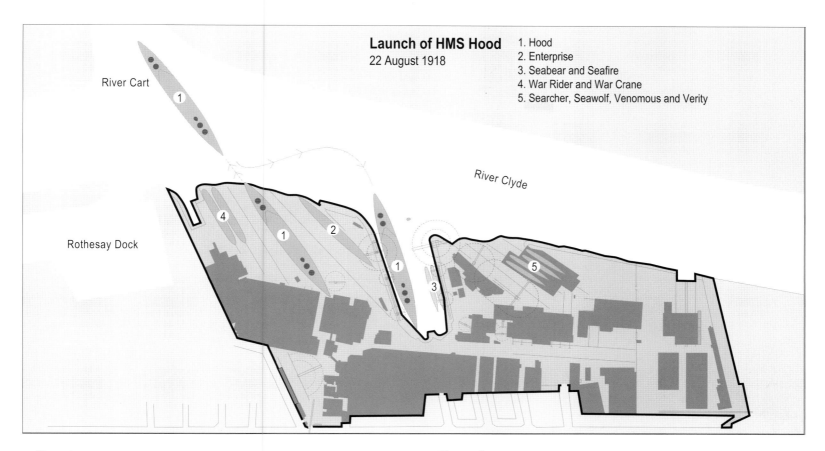

Launch of HMS Hood
22 August 1918

1. Hood
2. Enterprise
3. Seabear and Seafire
4. War Rider and War Crane
5. Searcher, Seawolf, Venomous and Verity

River Cart

Rothesay Dock

River Clyde

Structure

Complete up to and including the forecastle deck except for openings to ship machinery. There is no structure above forecastle deck except for the plating behind the armour of the conning tower and the after screen bulkhead. Roller paths and supports have not yet been placed in 'B' and 'X' barbettes.

Bulge

Complete with tubes and closed up except for the two forward compartments (one on each side) which were empty. Fashion plates cannot be fitted until the lower tier of side armour is complete.

Armour

Armoured bulkheads complete.

'A' and 'Y' barbettes complete.

'B' barbette complete except for 3 plates above the forecastle deck.

'X' barbette complete to upper deck, top tier of armour still to go on. No portion of revolving weight yet in place.

Conning Tower; only the lowest tier of armour below forecastle deck is on.

Side armour; nothing on except two plates (No 16 and 17) on the starboard side.

Machinery

Boilers complete except for some brickwork and lagging.

Main machinery not yet on board but most of auxiliary machinery is on board.

Electrical

Ring main fitted and about one-third of the electric cables are on board and being fitted.

General

Oil fuel and heating – all on board.

Air pipes and oil fuel seven-eighths on board.

Pumping flooding and draining seven-eighths on board.

350 and 100-ton pumps all on board.

50-ton and RW pumps only one on board.

Voice pipes three-quarters on board.

Scupper pipes, one-quarter on board.

Wood planking on weather portion of upper deck nearly complete none yet on forecastle deck.

Sheet iron work generally about 60 tons on board.

On 18 October 1918, with the War reaching its conclusion, the shipbuilder was told that it was the Admiralty's intention to decelerate some warship construction in their yard in favour of merchant work from this time onwards. List A was the priority for ships presently under construction and List B for the ships likely to be cancelled.

List A in order of priority:

1. *Hood, Enterprise, Seafire, Searcher* and *Seawolf*
2. *Sesame, Venom, Verity, Veteran* and *Vigo*
3. *Wistful* and *Virulent*

The shipyard was told that it was essential there should be no delay in the delivery of *Hood, Enterprise, Seafire, Searcher* and *Seawolf*.

List B

Volage and *Volcano*

These ships were to be stopped immediately and were later cancelled.

With the end of the First World War in November, the urgency that surrounded *Hood*'s completion ended. However, *Hood* and her three sister-ships did represent the latest British capital ships and viewed against the large warship building programmes undertaken by the Japanese and US navies, the issue was of importance. At the Board of the Admiralty meeting of 26 December 1918, the three sister-ships were discussed within this broader context as well as noting the implications for large warship construction at home if they were cancelled.

Question of completing Anson, Howe and Rodney.

It has been pointed out by Messrs Cammell Laird & Co in whose yard Howe is laid down, that the berth on which she has been commenced was specially equipped at a large cost and is the most important in their yard, that it is a serious matter for the berth to continue to stand idle now that ample labour is available, and that unless the work on Howe is proceeded with, compensation will be claimed until the berth is available for merchant shipbuilding.

The First Sea Lord informed the Board that the Chancellor of the Exchequer had intimated that it was assumed that the Admiralty would not proceed with new construction at the present time. He pointed out the difficulty in coming to any decision with regard to completing the three battle cruisers until more definite information is available as to the intentions of the United States of America in regard to their naval programme.

It was generally agreed that, but for the United States programme which had been foreshadowed, there would not be any strong argument for proceeding with the construction of these ships, and it was felt that in any case until the exact nature of any international arrangements that may be made at the Peace Conference are ascertained, it would be impossible to obtain Cabinet approval to proceed with the construction of ships each of which will cost not less than 5,750,000. The view was expressed that in any event it might be better to take up the ships at once in order to set free the berths and so that, should it be necessary to lay down other ships of this Class, a fresh design embodying the results of recent experience might be adopted. On the other hand it was pointed out that this would leave a gap of practically five years in the construction of large ships. It was agreed that a memorandum should be forwarded to the War Cabinet setting forth the whole position in order to obtain a cabinet decision as to the policy to be adopted.

The decision about their future had still not been made and on 7 February 1919, in a letter to both Cammell Laird and Fairfield, the position was still unclear:

I am commanded by My Lords Commissioners of the Admiralty to inform you that the question of proceeding with work on HMS Howe [and Rodney] has again been under consideration and it has been decided that all hull work including work on hull-subcontracts is to remain stopped for the present. It has also been decided that work on the main and auxiliary machinery and all work in connection with the main and auxiliary machinery for this ship is to be stopped for the present.

However, the fate of these ships was close to resolution as the Board meeting of 27 February made clear:

… having regard to all the circumstances the Board agreed that the construction of HM ships Anson, Howe and Rodney should forthwith be cancelled and the slips set free for merchant ship construction, and that in communicating this decision to the War Cabinet it should be made clear that the question of building additional battle cruisers will be reconsidered at the earliest possible moment after the terms of peace are finally settled; as unless further battle cruisers are built in the near future we shall before long fall behind the United States Navy in ships of that class …

As the incomplete hulls of the three sister-ships were dismantled on their building slips, further piecemeal additions were made to *Hood*. In May 1919, the Board approved the fitting of 2in protective plating on the main deck at the sides by the forward and after magazines. It had been found that at a certain angle of descent, the new 15in shell could enter *Hood* immediately above the 12in belt, through the 7in armour and reach the 15in magazines. To compensate for this additional weight, it was decided to remove the four after 5.5in guns which had already been fitted. Less critically but equally important for the shipbuilder was the location of the boat crutches on the boat deck. The ship's complement of boats had been decided in April and, as fitted as a flagship, the shipbuilder was informed that this was to be:

2 x 50' steam picket boat
1 x 45' motor launch (with auxiliary sails and oars)
2 x 32' sailing cutter
1 x 30' gig
2 x 27' whaler
2 x 16' skiff dinghy
2 x 13.5' balsa
1 x 45' barge
1 x 30' gig
1 x 25' motor boat

The only recorded fatalities during the construction of *Hood* occurred on 19 May 1919, when two men were killed and a number injured in an explosion in a compartment underneath the Carpenters' Heavy Store low down in the after part of the ship. The compartment, which had been completed and passed by Admiralty overseers early in March, had been cleared of all bilge water and thoroughly dried and then sealed. It had been opened again three weeks prior to the explosion and then again to air the compartment two days prior to the men entering. After the explosion, the body of one man was found on the floor of the Carpenters' Store. At the Fatal Accident Enquiry held in July, the shipyard manager, William Luke, said that the floor of the carpenters' store was 'tremendously torn up' pointing to a serious explosion. Mindful of possible sabotage, the compartment was tested by HM Factories Inspectors for traces of high explosive such as lyddite and amatol although none was found. Although gas was suspected, no cause was found and the explosion remained a mystery.

Between July and November, the long-awaited 15in mountings, that had held back progress for so long, were finally completed at Barrow and transported to Clydebank on the adapted coaster SS *Horden*. With the rest of the ship more or less complete, this enabled completion by the end of 1919. To enable her to leave the yard at the earliest date as, like *Australia*, *Hood* had overstayed her welcome, it was agreed that final touches to her armament would be carried out at Rosyth. On Friday 9 January 1920, the not-quite-complete *Hood* left John Brown's shipyard for the first and last time.

Her departure on a weekday precluded a large number of spectators but one reporter from the local newspaper, the Lennox Herald, became the first of many to comment on the handsome lines of this ship:

By noon, when preparations were starting for moving the great ship, the weather, which had been bright and frosty in the morning, took a change for the worse and snow began to fall.

Prompt to time, the four tugs at the stern of the Hood began towing the great vessel into the channel, and within fifteen minutes the warship was clear of the dock. There was a brief blink of sunshine at this stage and as Hood lay out clear of the land she presented an impressive picture in the bright light. Once the warship was safely in the river, two tugs which had been towing astern joined the pair at the stem of the vessel, and a few minutes after one, the journey down the river began. One of the tugs was being towed stern foremost at the stern of the big vessel, while the remaining tug stood by to render assistance if needed. A few seconds later, the Hood, having gathered way, gave three ear-piercing blasts on her syren as a farewell to Clydebank and the journey to the sea began.

From a vantage-point further down the river he continued:

Far away, the Hood was broadside on, and showed to perfection the long low lines of the hull, with the great powerful thrust of the bow, and the cut away cruiser stern, lines as graceful as those of a warship can be. The best picture of all however, was the three-quarter silhouette shown as the ship swung into the winding channel. The massive upperworks on the foredeck, from the great guns to the navigating turret, were then in the eye presenting a magnificent spectacle.

The shipyard description of the departure event and subsequent days was perfunctory:

This vessel was taken safely down river of 9 January. On Saturday she carried out a satisfactory preliminary trial, working up to over 130,000hp and on Monday, she left for Rosyth arriving there at mid-day on Tuesday 13th. Hood was safely drydocked on Tuesday 20 January and it is anticipated she will have her guns completed and leave Rosyth for Official Trials that will commence on 8 or 9 March.

Constructor Stanley Goodall, later to become the DNC, was on board *Hood* as she made her passage around the north of Scotland. He wrote this initial assessment of the ship under the heading 'Hood at Sea' once she had reached Rosyth.

The following remarks are submitted as a result of observations taken during the voyage from the Clyde to the Firth of Forth on January 12 and 13th :-

Seaworthiness.
After rounding the Mull of Kintyre, the sea was choppy with a moderate beam swell, waves were judged to be about 15-feet high, a strong wind, about force 8 was blowing from the west. A good deal of water was taken over the forecastle, some of this washed over the forward breakwater. 'A' barbette was continually deluged by spray. The pitching period was about 9 secs.

Off Islay, the ship rolled to about 3.75° (max) from the upright, water occasionally washed over the upper deck just abaft the break of forecastle. Rolling period was about 17 secs.

(Note. The ship was comparatively light, mean draught about 29'-10"; hence if, in any new design, less freeboard is accepted than that of 'Hood', we must be prepared for complaints that the vessel is wet)

The expansion joint at the shelter deck was opening about ?" while the ship was pitching. A fair amount of water came down the deck pipes into the cable locker, the bonnets did not appear efficient. The sickbay skylight leaked and several French mushroom tops let in water. Some need turning in order that the openings may be more sheltered (Mr Meryon is attending to this).

Vibration
The ship's speed did not exceed 21 knots and nowhere was the vibration of the structure at all noticeable except at the fore end of the 15" spotting top, where the overhang is considerable. The Commanding Officer said that at 28 knots the vibration in this position was excessive. If this is concurred in, Rosyth might be able to do something before full power trials.

The standard compass and Pelorus vibrated appreciably. Both these platforms should have some additional stiffening, but in my opinion, the standards of the instruments themselves are not sufficiently rigid and it is considered that this should be pointed out to DCD.

Bridge
The manoeuvring platform was too draughty, the currents were traced out and found to be thus:-
(there is a small sketch here – which I have)
The following alterations are considered necessary to effect an improvement :-
wings should be built on each side.
The canopy should be extended to the Pelorus Platform.
The canopy should be given a lip round the opening for the standard compass to reflect currents from this opening.
A canvas screen should be fitted round the standard compass as far as is permissible without obstructing the view to certain instruments.
(Note. In any future design it is for consideration whether a model of the bridge should not be tried in a wind tunnel to avoid complaints of draughts)

Machinery
Eng. Commander Woods of Messrs John Brown & Co stated that the water consumption was 11.4 lbs. per shp per hour for all purposes and the oil fuel consumption 20 tons per hour at 20 knots. These figures are given with all reserve.

The engine room ventilation was good, the usual repugnance of

Left: The after section showing bulkheads, held in place at this stage by wires, under erection in the forward, middle and after engine rooms (bulkheads BH217, BH239 and BH259). Further aft the port inner shaft is being fitted. The light wooden template forward and to the right of the shaft is lifting off the exact shape to allow a plate to be cut in the plater's shed. 'X' magazine is aft of bulkhead 259 and is the general area that would be devastated twenty-four years later. (Author's collection)

Right: A detail showing the hull up to the level of the main deck. The camera is directed at the after side of watertight bulkhead 217, which separated 'Y' boiler room from the forward engine room. Seatings for machinery can be seen in the engine room. The two men with arms interlocked are probably trying to talk to one another over the noise. (Author's collection)

134 • Ship No.460: *Hood*

Above: The quarterdeck showing work proceeding on 'X' barbette. 'Y' barbette has been completed. (Author's collection)

Left: A Yarrow water tube boiler being lowered into position directly above 'A' boiler room forward of watertight bulkhead 154. The first boiler is already in position below. Steel 'A' frames have been stepped on either side above the boiler room to lift the boiler, which weighed approximately 40 tons. (Author's collection)

Right: *Hood's* great length necessitated extending No 3 berth over the yard road and railway. Only the upper strakes of plating of the bow remain to be completed. The hull is a mass of painted marks in a variety of colours denoting instructions to riveters and platers. The number of rivets driven by each rivet squad were also marked off as squads were paid on a piecework system (by the number of rivets driven). (Author's collection)

Below: A view over the conning tower, 'B' and 'A' barbettes with the beams of the forecastle in place beyond that. An armoured plate for 'B' barbette is being moved into position. Note the compressed air line running along the deck providing power to rivet guns, caulking guns and drills. (Author's collection)

Left: A view along the forecastle deck looking forward taken after a fall of rain on 27 June 1918. Some deck plates are marked 'loose' and temporarily left un-riveted to enable machinery to be lowered to the decks below. (Author's collection)

Right: Only when the staging has been removed can the fine lines of the ship be seen. (Author's collection)

Below: Carpenters are planking the quarterdeck with 3in-thick teak. They lay teak around the cast steel bollard which is bolted to the steel deck and structure below. The metal structure over 'Y' barbette is there only to support a canvas cover should it rain. (Author's collection)

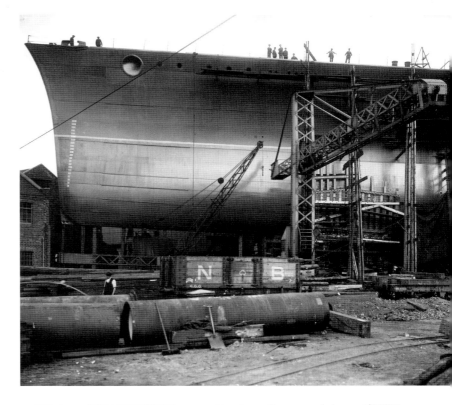

Right: *Hood*'s graceful bow photographed on 20 August 1918 rising above the shipyard buildings. The completed hull now clear of all staging is being prepared for launching. Bundles of drag chains have been arranged down either side of the slipway and attached to the ship's side on temporary fixings. The wires in the foreground keep the 5-ton lattice derrick cranes in position. (Author's collection)

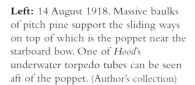

Left: 14 August 1918. Massive baulks of pitch pine support the sliding ways on top of which is the poppet near the starboard bow. One of *Hood*'s underwater torpedo tubes can be seen aft of the poppet. (Author's collection)

Left: 9 August 1918. A machinery set for one shaft comprising a high and low pressure turbine and the main gear wheel in the erecting shop. The crude heavy cast casing belies the sophisticated precision gearing inside. This set is ready for light steaming to take place and provide preliminary indication of any problems. Various oil feed lines can be seen supplying bearings etc. The shaft of the main gear wheel is emerging from the casing at right. This machinery set weighs many hundreds of tons and will subsequently be dismantled and taken in more manageable loads to the fitting-out basin for lifting into the ship. (Author's collection)

Right: The after end photographed on 19 August 1918 showing the arrangement of shafts, shaft brackets and propellers. (Author's collection)

Far Right: 22 August 1918. An unusual view of the starboard inner propeller and its shaft bracket which is riveted to the stern frame. (Author's collection)

Above: A detailed view of the starboard side forward on 22 August 1918, the day *Hood* was launched. Drag chains have been carefully arranged down the ship's side connected to the hull by wire ropes secured to temporary fixings. The dark painted recessed areas are where the belt armour will be bolted once the ship is in the water. (Author's collection)

Right: A view over the East Yard and its five building slips with the fitting-out basin and 150-ton derrick crane in the foreground. *Hood* dominates the scene on No 3 slip. Many items destined for *Hood* await her on the quayside. No 4 slip was the largest, capable of taking ships up 1000 feet in length. The longest ship built in the yard up to this time was the Cunard liner *Aquitania* at 901 feet overall. (Author's collection)

Left: 9 August 1918. One of four built-up, double helical main gear wheels (one for each shaft) in the engine shop at Clydebank. The gear wheel, with drive shaft visible, is sitting on blocks to be balanced. This gear wheel weighs something in the region of 50 to 60 tons. (Author's collection)

Right: A good view of the after portion of the hull showing *Hood*'s fine lines, the armour recess and the anti-torpedo bulge. The timber props supporting the hull will be removed before the launch. (Author's collection)

Below: *Hood*'s stern and the four propellers soon to be driven by the most powerful machinery so far installed in any ship. (Author's collection)

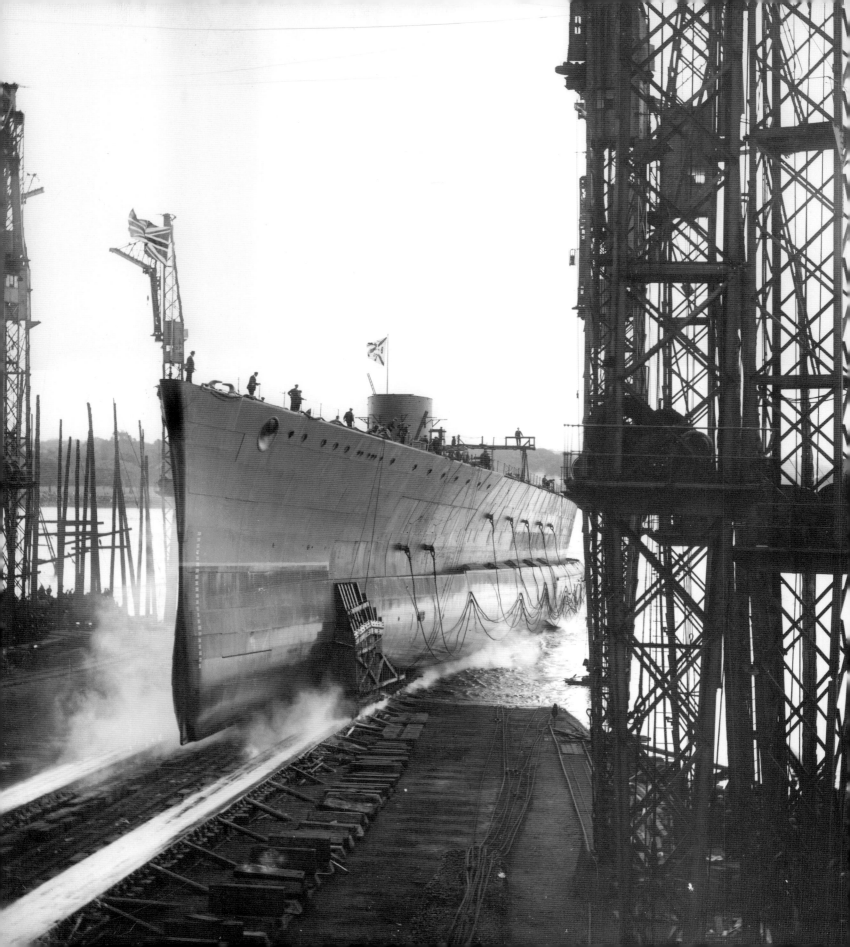

Left: Launch day, 22 August 1918, and *Hood* has travelled her own length down the slipway and is almost afloat. The wire ropes connecting the drag chains to the hull can be clearly seen. The upper portion of the bulges has yet to be fitted and faired into the ship's side. (Author's collection)

Right: *Hood*'s very fine lines are visible for the first time in the water. John Brown's house flag and the Union Jack are flying. (Author's collection)

Below: Attended by seven tugs, *Hood* has been brought to a rest after a short launching run across the Clyde into the mouth of the River Cart. (Author's collection)

Left: The ship at her fitting-out berth where she will remain for over 16 months. At the time of her launch over 2500 men were directly employed building the ship, many of whom were in the shops. (Author's collection)

Right: A detail of the midships area showing the lower half of a gear case, one of four, being lowered into one of the engine rooms. This gear case will eventually contain the drive shaft from the main gear wheel and the reduction gearing which will drive the propeller shaft. (Author's collection)

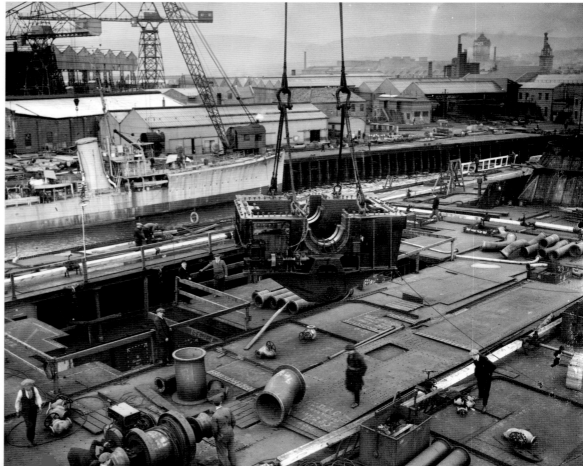

Above: 12 September 1918. Two armoured plates for 'B' barbette being lifted on board. 'A' barbette had been completed prior to her launch. All armour plates have previously been keyed together in the armour erecting shops. Both plates in this shot show the grooves down the edge where they will be keyed together. The ring bulkhead for 'B' barbette has been erected. The armour plates will be bolted to this structure through holes visible on the ring bulkhead. (Author's collection)

Above left: The mainmast complete with stanchions, rails and ladders is lifted on board. Photograph taken on 2 May 1919. (Author's collection)

Above right: The foremast with starfish, torpedo and searchlight platforms already fitted is lifted on board. The after funnel has been erected. (Author's collection)

Right: The upper portion of the bulge has been framed and plating is in progress. Much of the side armour has been fitted while abreast of 'A' turret a plate is being fitted, having been lifted off the pontoon. (Author's collection)

Left: The stern showing the freshly painted interiors of 'X' and 'Y' barbettes. Note the aftermost 5.5in mountings have already been fitted but will subsequently be removed before completion of the ship to compensate for the addition of extra armour. (Author's collection)

Right: Work is proceeding closing up the bulges while a condenser sitting on the quayside is being rigged for lifting into the engine room through one of the large openings on the upper deck. (Author's collection)

Left: A good view of the fitting-out basin with the East Yard beyond. With *Hood* in the fitting-out basin are three destroyers at various stages of completion and the standard ship *Bata* or *War Crane*. The photograph was taken from the roof of the Boiler Shops probably on a Sunday as Sunday work was discontinued at the request of the Admiralty. Not a single person appears in the shot. (Author's collection)

Above: As work on the bulges continues, it is just possible to see the crushing tubes fitted into each bulge compartment. Work on the bridge structure is well advanced and 5.5in mounting P1 is in place. The 'Modified W' class destroyers *Verity* and *Veteran* and a Standard type merchant ship are also fitting-out. (Author's collection)

Above: In this photograph taken on 4 July 1919, the control top has been erected on the foremast starfish. Many plates have yet to be fitted on the boat deck while those that are in place are bolted only and not as yet riveted. Note the large boiler room vents on either side of the funnels. The garland is in honour of the wedding day of Engineering Commander Sydenham – possibly an Admiralty overseer. (Author's collection)

Right: The side armour is in place as are all of the forward 5.5in mountings. With scant regard for their safety at least 16 workmen and a naval officer are working on the control top. The vessels in the foreground are the passenger ferries *Antwerp* and *Bruges* under construction for the Great Eastern Railway Co. (Author's collection)

Left: An untypical photograph taken of workmen waiting for the whistle at the end of the working day (5.15pm) on 28 August 1919. Workmen were rarely the primary subject of photographs which suggests this one was taken for a management issue. (Author's collection)

Right: 7 August 1919. The first 15in gun being lowered into position on 'X' turret. (Author's collection)

Left: A later view with 'X' and 'Y' turrets ostensibly complete. On the after end of the shelter deck the searchlight platform and torpedo control tower are now complete and the 4in high angle guns are in place. Painting the ship is in progress. The cruiser *Enterprise* is taking shape in the background. (Author's collection)

Right: The late delivery of *Hood*'s main armament from Barrow delayed completion of the ship. With the exception of 'A' and 'B' turrets and the 15in director on the conning tower, the ship appears to be otherwise externally complete in this photograph taken in November 1919. 'A' turret roof armour has yet to be fitted while 'B' turret awaits its gun shields and roof armour. *Antwerp* was not completed until May 1920 and *Bruges* in September 1920. (Author's collection)

Below: The gun shields and roofs of 'A' and 'B' turrets are now complete. The 30ft rangefinder has been fitted on the main armament director while minor work is underway completing 'B' turret. (Author's collection)

The following series of photographs of the completed ship were taken on the morning of 9 January 1920 shortly before the ship left Clydebank.

Above: A good midships view. Draught marks below the refuse chute indicate 28 feet. (Author's collection)

Right: The Mk II gun turrets, massive conning tower and imposing bridgework. (Author's collection)

Left: Note the plating detail and line of the armoured belt. The range clocks are just visible under the starfish and to the side of the torpedo lookout position. (Author's collection)

Above: Note the size of the 32ft rangefinder on top of the 15in director and the voice tubes running horizontally under the fore bridge. There is also some indication of the system of ladderways at the rear of the bridge. (Author's collection)

Right: Note the arrangement of plating strakes at the bow and the thickness of the plates. The curved fitting suspended from the bow is the bar shoe for the paravane gear. (Author's collection)

Left: Note the fine run of the armoured belt into the hull and the Carley floats by 'Y' turret. (Author's collection)

Above: Starboard 5.5in mountings and the 32ft cutter sitting askew on its davits. Note the number of swinging booms fitted to the ship in this area. (Author's collection)

Left: The bridge structure, foremast and control top is complete with the exception of the 15in director which was fitted at Rosyth. (Author's collection)

Right: Immediately abaft the mainmast is the searchlight control platform with the night defence control position underneath. (NRS UCS1-118-460-464)

Above: Note the two covering plates over the torpedo tubes that were removed from the ship after launching. Because of delays in her completion and urgency in getting her to Rosyth, *Hood* never received her final coat of paint at Clydebank, as evident in this photograph. (NRS UCS1-118-460-464)

Left: An excellent view across the midships area. Deck planks have been stored on the forecastle deck to the left of the 5.5in mountings; planking has not been completed in that area. The ferry *Antwerp* and recently launched cruiser *Enterprise* are lying at the other side of the fitting-out basin. (NRS UCS1-118-460-454)

Right: The forecastle in December 1919. Note the paravane houses built into the structure of the breakwater. The ship in the background is the *St Denis*, built at Clydebank as *Munich* in 1908 for the Great Eastern Railway Co. (NRS UCS1-118-460-460)

Left: A detail of the photograph on page 169 showing personnel watching the photographer on the starboard side of the shelter deck. The 15ft torpedo control rangefinder, W/T office and searchlight platform is behind them. (Author's collection)

Right and Below: Two wonderfully atmospheric images of *Hood* being carefully manoeuvred out of the fitting-out basin in the early afternoon of 9 January 1920. (Author's collection)

Left: Eleven years after the first battlecruiser, *Inflexible*, made the same journey, *Hood*, the last battlecruiser and a ship twice the size, is pulled into the river channel to make her way to the sea. (NRS UCS1-118-460-478)

Right: A detail of the doors covering the torpedo tubes on the starboard side.

Below: With John Brown's West Yard covered berths in the foreground and Newshot Isle to the left, *Hood* is approaching the large shipbuilding works of William Beardmore & Co at Dalmuir. With four tugs ahead and two astern, this is the beginning of a ten-mile passage down the Clyde to the Tail of the Bank. (Author's collection)

Above, Above Right and Right:
Hood was at Rosyth Dockyard until March 1920 for minor adjustments and where the 15in director tower was fitted on the control top and flying-off platforms fitted on 'B' and 'X' turrets. This and the photograph below and opposite show the ship running trials off Arran, probably full power trials, on 18 March 1920. During this run, *Hood* developed a mean of 151,280shp for a mean speed of 32.07 knots on a displacement of 42,200 tons. (Author's collection)

Left: *Hood* heels to port during turning trials. Her quarterdeck was notoriously wet but not sufficiently so in this shot to deter one hardy individual standing at the stern. (NRS UCS1-118-460-489)

THE 'G3' BATTLECRUISERS

Clydebank's association with battlecruisers did not end with *Hood*. Driven by the need to maintain its position in the face of new construction in the United States and Japan, the Admiralty worked on a series of designs for completely new battlecruisers and battleships. By September 1921, 48,000-ton battlecruisers known by their design prefix 'G3', were ready to proceed. The tendering process followed the pre-war pattern as the various Admiralty departments swung into administrative action.

Invitations to tender were issued to shipbuilders on 1 September with the specified date for submission of completed tenders no later than 'noon, Saturday 1st of October', subsequently extended until 8 October. Drawings and specifications were made available to view for the tendering shipbuilders between 2 and 15 September. Attached to the letter of invitation was a document of twenty-one separate points of information concerning the ships to be built, one of which stated that Establishment Charges and Profit would be £700,000 not subject to alteration. For economical construction, the Admiralty offered to pay a bonus to the shipbuilder whose price was below the average price of all four completed ships. As before, the Admiralty would supply armour; anchors, cables and ship's boats; electrical machinery; lamp fittings, searchlights and radiators etc.; gun mountings, guns and torpedo tubes. The Admiralty also gave the time in months for delivery to shipyards of the roller paths, training racks, steam pumping engines, shell room gear and turrets associated with the ship's armament. Because weights to be lifted were heavier than before, shipbuilders were told that deck plates would weigh up to 35 tons, armour plates up to 40 tons and the armament up to a maximum of 185 tons. Shipbuilders were required to have the requisite means of lifting these loads. The ships were to be completed in thirty-six months.

On 7 October John Brown & Co submitted their tender which included several provisions, one of which concerned the 36-month construction period. While they were confident in meeting this deadline, the shipbuilders expressed the possibility of unforeseen difficulties in the electric welding of the armour deck 'with which we are not yet familiar'.

On 24 October, John Brown & Co was advised that they had been provisionally awarded a contract to build one of the ships the other three being placed with Beardmore, Fairfield and Swan Hunter & Wigham Richardson. The indications are that John Brown & Co was intended as the lead yard. Considerable attention and interest appears to have been paid to the proposed machinery installation for the battlecruisers and at the end of October, Admiral Dixon visited Clydebank with the machinery overseer, Commander Gurnell, to meet with Commander W H Wood, Manager of the Clydebank engine works.

On 3 November, the Admiralty provided the shipyard with the following drawings:

Hull structural
Hull general
Electric high power
Electric low power
Rig
Electric generators etc.
Capstan
Completion
Electrically-driven boat hoists

Drawings (tables) of the offsets were also provided to enable the ship to be laid off. The Admiralty requested that Brown's pass these sheets on as quickly as possible to Fairfield, Beardmore and Swan Hunter & Wigham Richardson.

A conference was held on 11 November at the Admiralty to discuss the ship's machinery – principally the type of turbines to be used and

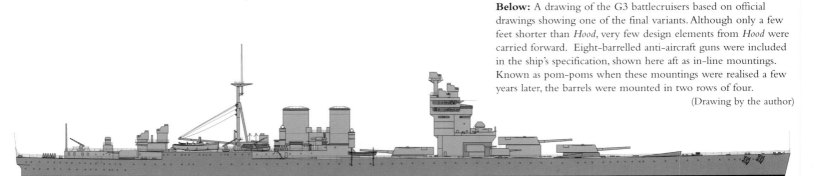

Below: A drawing of the G3 battlecruisers based on official drawings showing one of the final variants. Although only a few feet shorter than *Hood*, very few design elements from *Hood* were carried forward. Eight-barrelled anti-aircraft guns were included in the ship's specification, shown here aft as in-line mountings. Known as pom-poms when these mountings were realised a few years later, the barrels were mounted in two rows of four.

(Drawing by the author)

other engineering issues. At 160,000shp, this installation was the most powerful so far proposed by the Admiralty and well in excess of *Hood's* 144,000shp Brown-Curtis installation.

A letter dated 14 November, advised the shipbuilder that the following companies would be responsible for supplying the armour for their ship:

560lbs belt	Brown
480lbs belt	Armstrong
Funnel protection	Brown
Upper deck	Brown
Lower deck	Brown
200lbs bulkhead	Vickers
480lbs bulkhead	Armstrong
400lbs bulkhead	Armstrong
160lbs bulkhead	Vickers
'A' barbette	Vickers
'B' barbette	Brown
'X' barbette	Cammell Laird

While these events were in train, the major naval powers met in Washington on 11 November to find a way of stopping what was in effect a new arms race which, for the British at least, would have been financially ruinous given the post-war financial position. On 16 November, the Admiralty informed the shipbuilders that the contracts were suspended pending the outcome of the conference. Despite the suspension, certain aspects of the design of the machinery were allowed to proceed and on 17 November, the Engineer-in-Chief invited engineering personnel from John Brown to a conference on 22 November to consider purely design arrangements of the ship's machinery. Further machinery specifications were passed to the shipbuilder on 25 November under the proviso that this should not be taken as an instruction to proceed.

Three weeks later, on 6 December, the Admiralty wrote to the shipbuilder saying that any expense incurred relative to the ship's machinery was to be confined to turbine design arrangements, boiler design, feed arrangements, condenser evacuating arrangements and turbine drive for circulating pumps. Details were not to be considered and no expense was to be incurred with sub-contractors. Three days later a further instruction asked that drawing office and experimental work be carried out in the following areas:

Tests of electrically-welded deck plates.
Full-sized test of a double bottom tank to determine the suitability of framing and frame spacing.
Theoretical investigation into the strength of the main transverse and longitudinal bulkheads.
Design work in connection with special fittings such as hatchway covers and similar arrangements to protect openings in the thick armour deck including the making of samples of such fittings for tests.
Design of shaft brackets.

By February 1922, the Washington Conference had reached agreement with the decision that the construction plans of the US, Japanese and British navies should be brought to an end. Unlike the lingering indecision that surrounded *Hood's* three sister-ships, the fate of the 'G3s' would be mercifully brief – they were cancelled outright on 21 February 1922. The letter from the Admiralty to the shipbuilder said unequivocally that 'it has been definitely decided that no further work is to be proceeded with…'. Costs associated with the contract were requested for payment. The costs as submitted by the shipbuilder in March were as follows:

Hull

Labour expended until 19 Nov	£892
Material	2,715
Proportion of Establishment Charges (£520,000) (25 days out of three years)	11,872
Labour and material expended subsequent to 19 Nov	758
Less scrap of	594
Total	**15,644**

Additionally –	
Colvilles steel plates and sections	7,587
Plus pitch pine piles and keel blocks	
Total	**7,672**
Total Hull	**23,316**

Machinery

Labour expended until 19 Nov	1,190
Material	451
Proportion of Establishment Charges (£180,000) (25 days out of three years)	4,109
Total	**5,750**
Expended since 19 Nov	
Labour	389
Material	2
Establishment Charges at 50%	194
Profit % 7.5%	44
Total	**6,381**

Additionally to A Cohen for cancellation of contract for gunmetal	2,279
Total Machinery	**8,660**
Final Total	**£31,976**

On 5 April 1922 the last act in the 'G3' contract saga was the return of all drawings and hull and machinery specifications to the Admiralty. Fifteen years would pass before another capital ship, the battleship *Duke of York* was laid down at Clydebank.

APPENDICES

1. Comparisons

As built particulars*

	Inflexible	Australia	Tiger	Repulse	Hood
Displacement (tons)					
Load	17,290	18,500	28,430	26,854	42,670
Deep	20,700	21,240	33,260	31,592	46,680
Dimensions (feet)					
Length oa	567	590	704	794 2'5"	860 7"
pp	530	555	660	750	810 5"
Beam					
Extreme	78' 10"	79' 11"	90' 6"	89' 11.5"	105' 2.5"
Depth					
Moulded	40' 6"	41' 3.5"		49' 1"	50' 6"
Draught (mean)					
Load	25' 10.5"	25' 10.5"	28' 5"	25' 9.5"	29' 3"
Deep	29' 9"		32' 5"	29' 8"	32'
Machinery					
Boilers	31 Yarrow	31 B&W	39 B&W	42 B&W	24 Yarrow
Turbines	Parsons	Parsons	Brown-Curtis	Brown-Curtis	Brown-Curtis
Mean shp (trials, full power)	46,947	55,881	104,635	118,913	150,473
Mean speed (trials, full power)	26.48	26.89	29.07	31.73	31.79
Armament					
Main	8 x 12"BL MkX	8 x 12"BL MkX	8 x 13.5"BL MkV	6 x 15" BL MkI	8 x 15" BL MkI
Secondary	16 x 4" QFMkIII	16 x 4" QFMkIII	12 x 6" BL Mk VII	17 x 4" BL Mk IX	12 x 5.5 BL MkI
AA	-	2 x 3" Mk I	2 x 3" MkI	2 x 3" MkI	4 x 4" QF MkV
Torpedoes	5 x 18"	2 x 18"	4 x 21"	2 x 21"	6 x 21"
Armour					
Belt	6" and 4" fwd	6" and 4" ends	9" and 4" ends	6" and 4" fwd, 3" aft	12", 6", 5" fwd, 5" aft
Bulkheads	6"	4"	4"	7", 5" and 4"	5"
Barbettes	7"	7"	9" and 8'	7", 5" and 4"	12" and 10"
Conning Tower	10"sides, 3"roof	10" sides, 3" roof	10" sides, 3" roof	10" sides, 3" roof	11 to 7" sides, 5" roof
Turrets	7" walls, 3" roof	7" walls, 3" roof	9" walls, 3.25" roof	9" walls, 4.25" roof	15 to 11" walls, 3" roof
Forecastle Deck	-	-	1" to 1.5"	0.75" to 1.5"	1.75" to 2"
Upper Deck	-	-	-	1" to 4"	0.75" to 2"
Main Deck	1" to 2"	1" to 2"	1" to 2"	1" to 2"	1" to 3"
Lower Deck	1.5" to 2.5"	1" to 2.5"	1" to 3"	1.75" to 2.5"	1" to 3"

*Based on data abstracted from Battlecruisers by John Roberts.

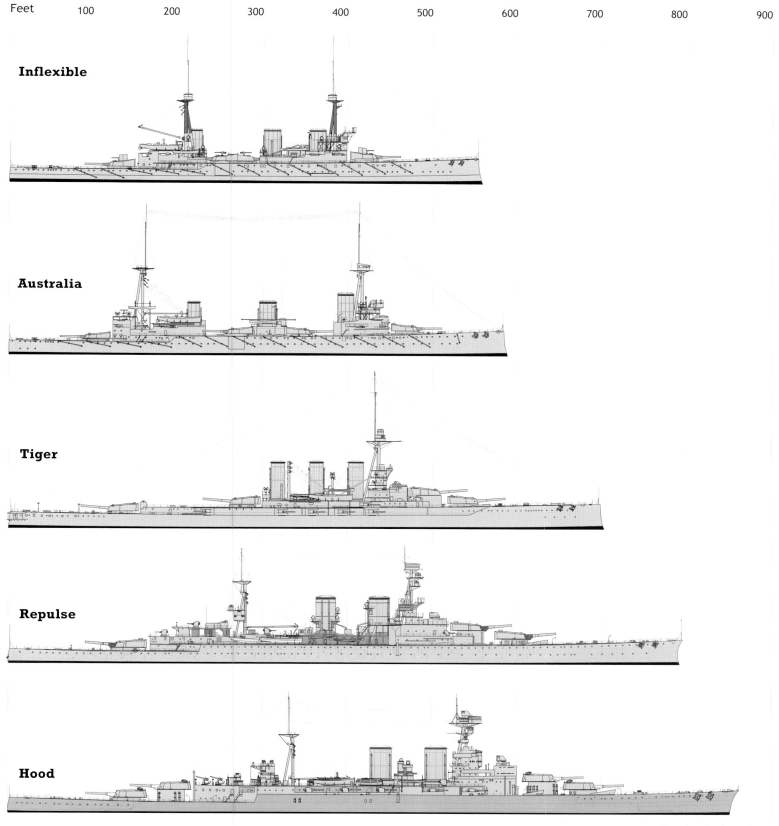

Feet 100 200 300 400 500 600 700 800 900

Inflexible

Australia

Tiger

Repulse

Hood

(Drawings by the author)

2. *Repulse* and *Hood*: Manpower Levels during Construction

HMS Hood
Construction Time
Shipyard manning levels
(excluding engines and boilers)

- Total of all trades
- Steel trades only (Ironworkers)

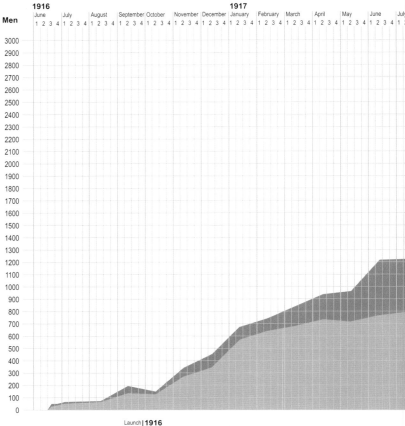

HMS Repulse
Construction Time
Shipyard manning levels
(excluding engines and boilers)

- Total of all trades
- Steel trades only (Ironworkers)

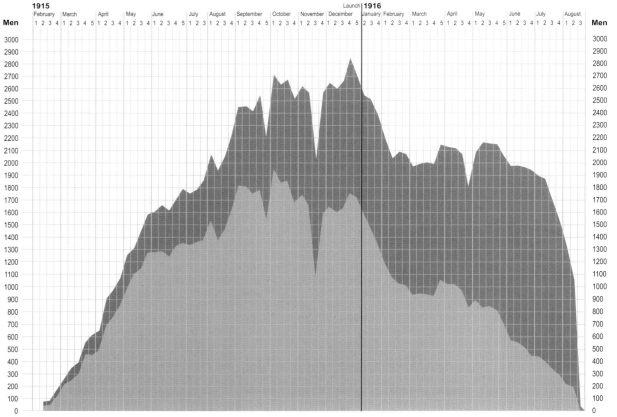

(Graphs by the author)

moulding loft and work on scrieve boards proceeding. Preparing principal moulds for casting. No mechanical work yet in hand owing to lack of material.

20 June

Keel laid. Framing commenced. Proceeding with work in Moulding Loft.

29 July

Keel erected on blocks and being riveted. Proceeding with frames. Docking keels and longitudinals. Mould loft work and armour moulds making good progress. All large steel castings ordered.

26 August

Keel 7/8ths erected and riveting well advanced. Docking keels being erected. Double bottom framing making progress in shop and a good start made with the erecting of frames and longitudinals. Lower deck beams making good progress. Mould loft work proceeding on armour moulds.

24 September

Double bottom framing proceeding. Commencement made to lower bottom plating: progress is slow due to want of material.

22 October

Framing to Lower Deck 7/8ths completed in shop. Framing to Lower Deck half erected at ship. Tank top plating progressing. Transverse bulkhead making good progress. Heel casting in place. Armour moulds well advanced, and all dispatched except Battery and Casemates. Preparing to commence outer bottom plating.

22 November

Shaft tube castings delivered. Framing in shop three-quarters complete. Framing three-quarters erected to Lower Deck. Inner bottom half plated. Lower Deck beams half erected. Platform Deck erected. Shell plating commenced. Riveting following close on plating.

18 December

Seven-eighths framed and beamed to Lower Deck. Inner bottom half plated and proportionally riveted. A good start made to shell plating. Bulkheads, deckplating and flats being prepared in shops. Stem casting erected.

1913

22 January

Shell, Lower and Main Deck plating being proceeded with. Inner bottom plating seven-eighths completed. Shaft tubes making good progress. Two shaft brackets delivered. Bulkheads being erected. Bunker bulkheads prepared and ready for erecting.

19 February

Shaft tubes ready for ship. Riveting of inner and outer bottom being pushed on. Longitudinal bulkheads being erected. Boiler and engine seating commenced. Proceeding with plating and riveting of Lower Deck. Main Deck beams ready for ship, and Upper Deck beams and plating one half prepared.

28 March

Three-quarters shell plated below lower deck. Riveting following close up. Lower Deck plating making good progress, Bunker bulkheads erected. Magazine protection bulkheads being erected. Shaft tubes being put in place. Boiler stools and engine seats making good progress.

25 April

Three-quarters framing erected to Main Deck and a few frames erected to Forecastle Deck. Lower Deck three-quarters plated and riveting

following close up. Shell seven-eighths plated up to Lower Deck. Main Deck plating being erected and Forecastle Deck plating being prepared in shop. Shaft tubes being fixed in place. Internal work being well manned up. Commenced to fit No 298 Armour Bulkhead in ship.

26 May

Seven-eighths shell plated below Lower Deck and riveting following close up. Shaft tubes all in place. Two shaft brackets delivered and being erected. Lower Deck seven-eighths plated and a start made to Main Deck. Upper and Forecastle deck plating being prepared in shop. Internal iron work below Lower Deck making good progress.

25 June

Frames and beams being erected above Lower Deck. Shell plating behind armour progressing. Two shaft brackets secured in place. Water testing of double bottom making good progress. Engine and boiler bearers being riveted. Shell riveting below Lower Deck three-quarters completed.

16 July

No report.

28 August

Shell and deck plating from Engine Room aft being pushed on for boring out. Preparing boiler rooms for shipping boilers. Eleven side armour plates erected and all bulkhead armour in place except for four plates. Armour for X barbette being erected. Watertesting making good progress.

16 September

Good progress being made with water testing. Special efforts being made to plate and rivet shell and decks aft. Boilers being shipped. Engine bearers three-quarters completed. Lower belt of armour plates being erected.

15 October

Stern ready for engineers boring out. One half of watertesting below lower deck complete. All boilers on board. Lower Deck over boilers closed in. Main Deck plating complete. Upper Deck plating 7/8ths complete. Framing between Upper and Forecastle Decks ? complete. Lower strake of armour being fitted. Engine bearers almost completed.

21 November

Water testing ⅝ths done below Lower Deck: a good start made above Lower Deck. Engine bearers complete. All side armour plates (lower tier) fitted. Upper Deck plating complete. Forecastle Deck plating one-half complete. Boring out for stern shafts finished. First rudder in place; second rudder ready for erecting. Fitting of X barbette plates seven-eighths complete and Q barbette one-quarter complete. Side armour backing one-third complete.

22 December

Launched on 15 December.

Ship taken to fitting-out basin and moored under 150-ton West crane.

Staging ship's side for fitting armour plates. Preparing and fitting ironwork of barbettes. Mast shipped. Continuing water testing and pushing on with fan flats.

There are no monthly reports for *Repulse*.

4.4 HMS *Hood*

(Shipyard Monthly Reports resumed in January 1919)
Ship No 460, No 3 Berth, East Yard

1919

30 January

Satisfactory progress continues to be made with the hull and with the armour. A commencement has been made in closing in the decks and other structure over the forward engine room.

27 February

The second funnel has now been shipped on this vessel, also part of the conning tower, and a commencement has been made with the laying of planking on Forecastle Deck forward.

27 March

Good progress is being made with the fitting of side armour on this vessel, as also with the armoured wall of the conning tower. The bridge erections, which are of unusual dimensions, are now being erected on the ship. The fourth set of turbines will be steamed this week, and it is hoped to dismantle them and place them on board in the early part of April.

4 May

The fourth set of turbines has been shipped on board and good progress is being made with replacing the decks over same. The closing-in of the upper portion of the buoyancy tube space adjoining lowest strakes of armour is also proceeding satisfactorily.

29 May

Shipwrights are making good progress with Forecastle Deck planking. The decks are now closed up over fourth set of turbines and the erection of the Shelter Deck is making good progress.

26 June

The erection of side armour is now completed. The stowage of buoyancy tubes in anti-submarine bulges is completed on starboard side and 90% completed on port side. The pit trials have been successful and the first 15-inch mounting for Clydebank is promised by the 8th July.

31 July

The large anti-submarine compartments [bulges] of this ship were completed before stopping for the holidays, when the last strakes of plating on the port side were riveted up and caulked. The first pair of 15-inch mountings was completed at Vickers' Works early in July but they have not yet been able to deliver them at Clydebank owing to the difficulty in obtaining a ship for transporting same.

21 August

The first pair of 15" mountings are now erected on X barbette and the guns are in place. Messers Vickers have undertaken to deliver the second set of mountings for Y barbette in the beginning of September. Whenever these are in place it will be possible to proceed with the alignment of the machinery. Good progress has been made generally during the last fortnight thanks to the Peace Celebrations being confined to Monday 4th August.

3 September

As the result of reports to the Cabinet by Sir Joseph McLay and the Controller General of Merchant Shipbuilding, the Controller of the Navy, Sir William Nicholson and his staff, came to Clydebank on 8 August and discussed the question as to what expenditure of labour was involved in completing the 'Hood' at Clydebank, and what consequences would be involved as far as the completion of new Merchant work and reconditioning of vessels returned from the Navy to merchant work was concerned.

After discussion, the Controller requested me to write officially what I had said to him, for consideration by the Board of Admiralty, and as a result, we received notification from the Board of the Admiralty on 25 August intimating that work on HMS *Hood* could be proceeded with as per the penultimate paragraph of our letter on 8 August and work, therefore, is proceeding accordingly.

30 October

The second barbette, with guns complete, was erected on board the ship in the beginning of October, thus enabling the alignment of shafting and the setting up of main engines in place to be proceeded with. The additional protection plating over magazines has now been completed. Satisfactory progress is being made by the joiners and electricians in the living quarters of the ship.

27 November

Progress on all outside work during this past month has been seriously impeded owing to the most unusual severity of the weather for a full fortnight in the middle of this month, for not only was there heavy snow but the thermometer frequently registered in the middle of the day from 15 to 19 degrees of frost.

On *Hood*, the third barbette and guns are now erected on board, and the fourth barbette has just been delivered and a commencement has been made with the erection of same. Satisfactory progress is being made with all internal work, especially electrical work and ventilation. The rigging of masts and derricks is making good progress. Due to the weights being on board, the machinery has now been entirely set up and it is proposed to have a basin trial on 9 December.

A conference is being arranged for Friday 28 November as to whether the fitting of guns and other parts of the armament will admit of the ship leaving this yard on 9 January.

18 December

The fourth barbette with guns and gun shields is now erected on board. The basin trial of the engines took place on 9 and 19 December and it is now being officially arranged that the vessel shall leave Clydebank dock at mid-day on Friday 9 January.

5. *Tiger*: Armour and Other Weights (excluding machinery and armament)

Armour	Tons	Armour	Tons	Castings	
360lb side armour	1,117	120lb barbette armour	344	Stem	10
bolts	22	bolts and straps	32	Stern	37
240lb side armour	526	80lb on casemates	20	Shaft brackets	93
bolts	11	straps etc.	2	Shaft tubes	20
200lb side armour	960	400lb on conning and signal tower	59	Rudders	65
bolts	19	120lb roof plate	13	Total	225
160lb side armour	398	8lb floor plates to conning tower			
bolts	8	(including 160lb floor scuttles)	14	Remaining backing, hull etc.	8,400
120lb side armour	123	3in and 4in communication tubes	23	**Total**	**16,970**
bolts	3	240lb control tower	14		
200lb on casemates	50	120lb roof plate	4	This weight was exclusive of anchors, cables,	
200lb on bulkheads	45	80lb floor plates to control tower		boats, coal hoists, boat hoists, lifts to engine and	
bolts	1	(including 160lb floor scuttles)	6	boiler rooms, engine room fans, but inclusive of	
160lb on bulkheads	120	4in communication tube	6	capstan gear.	
bolts	3	80lb conning tower supports	34		
80lb bulkhead armour	14	straps etc.	3	**Anchors**	
straps	2	120lb auxiliary torpedo director hoods	8	3 x 150cwt stockless	
360 and 320lb barbette armour	430	**Total**	**4,495**	1 x 46cwt stockless	
bolts	5			4 x 6cwt kedge	
160lb barbette armour	52	High tensile plates and angles	3,850		
bolts and straps	4			**Cables**	
				500 fathoms of 3in	
				Weight of cables	125

6. Progressive Trials, HMS *Repulse*

Report received by DNC 15 September 1916. And circulated to First and Third Sea Lords.

I attended yesterday the progressive trials of HMS *Repulse* which were conducted off Arran. Double runs, with and against the tide, were made at 15, 20, 25, 30 knots and the maximum.

With the maximum power obtained a mean speed of 31 ? knots was obtained. This was very satisfactory as the vessel had a displacement of 29,900 tons on a mean draught of 28' 2 ?". She was complete with ammunition, stores etc, and had about two-thirds of her full fuel. The wind was very strong and varied from about 5 to 6 at the commencement of the trial to force 8 at the finish, which kept the ship back considerably when facing the wind.

The maximum horsepower on the full speed runs was about 119,000 which was not as much by about 6,000hp as was obtained on the full power runs made before she docked at Portsmouth.

The new course off Arran was considered very satisfactory, though on this particular occasion it was rather exposed to the wind from the North West.

The information obtained from these progressive runs is of very great value for present and future designs, as the results obtained were quite reliable.

7. Report on Behaviour of *Repulse* on Passage North

Letter from Captain Fuller to Rear Admiral Commanding, First Battle Cruiser Squadron.

Sir,
In accordance with H.F.178/76 of 6th November 1916 and with reference to the enclosure herewith, which gives the details of the bad weather, etc during the period in question, I have the honour to report that the general behaviour of Repulse in a considerable Atlantic sea was very good.

The ship had a steady and even motion, and the bow flare prevented seas breaking over the forecastle to a great extent, but as soon as the wind was able to free the spume from the curve of the ship's side, a large amount of spray was blown up and over the conning tower platform and admiral's bridge.

The pronounced flare combined with Repulse's light build, causes the fore end of the ship from A turret forward, to receive exceptionally severe blows when pitching in a heavy sea, and on the occasion under review, the forward deadlights gave way, whilst the oil tanks forward of 88 bulkhead commenced to leak.

When steaming at 12 knots and over against the head sea in question, the ship dipped her bow, on an average, into every third wave; and occasionally she shipped a considerable amount of water that resulted in the forecastle deck sinking about one inch for a distance of 16 feet in a weak place between the foremost fairleads and hawse pipes.

With the exception of the single mountings, the four-inch guns were suitably placed for rough weather.

As regards the engines, the movement of the ship was not sufficient to cause much racing.

From experience to date, it is considered that *Repulse* will make more progress against a heavy sea, than a ship of similar light build and freeboard, but without a flare to her forecastle. At the same time, when deciding on new construction with a flare, the bow should if anything be made stiffer.

This broadly satisfactory report drew the following response for the DNC's office:

The slight sinking of the forecastle deck reported occurred right forward between the hawse pipes, and additional pillaring as necessary has already been arranged for. The oil tanks at 88 bulkhead are in wake of A and B barbette, and it has been submitted to omit all oil from these tanks in both ships, in view of the weight of additional protection which has recently been approved for them. Separate enquiries have been made in regard to the giving away of the forward deadlights. It is not stated how the glass scuttles, which are 1 ?" thick, behaved. It is not clear what the term 'light build' used by the Commanding Officer, as the ship has heavy scantlings which are in proper proportion to her dimensions and type; for the Hood

Class, where the displacement is much increased, a closer spacing of frames is being adopted at the ends of the ship. [frame spacing made three feet instead of four feet]

As regards the flare, which is much in excess of any previous large ship, it is noticed that the Commanding Officer is of opinion that Repulse will make more progress against a heavy sea than a ship of similar freeboard but without the flare. The flare prevented seas breaking over the forecastle to a great extent, but did not prevent the wind blowing spray over the upper works of the ship as soon as it was able to free the spume from the ship's side. It has been submitted by DNC, dealing with the behaviour of large ships at sea, that is impossible to keep heavy seas and spray from breaking over the forecastle, more especially at any rate of speed, and as these cruisers are considerably faster than anything we have ever had before, in the way of big ships, the fact that the flare reduced the amount of water shipped, shows that it is advantageous to retain it.

In the Hood Class the same flare as *Repulse* has been shown on the sheer draught. If it be desired to somewhat reduce it, a tracing is herewith showing an alternative deck line which reduces the maximum flare by three feet. This could, if so desired, be adopted in, say two of the vessels of the class for comparison with the others.

8. Programme for Steaming *Hood*, March 1920.

SHP	Period	Remarks
9,000	3 hours	A. two forward sets of turbines with steam to cruising turbine only, two after sets of turbines with closed exhaust steam only.
"	3 hours	B. steam to cruising turbines only, after turbine sets running in vacuum.
1/10th power	3 hours	Under conditions A
14,500		
"	3 hours	Under conditions B
Maximum power obtainable with cruising turbines	3 hours	Under conditions A
1/5th power	3 hours	C. All turbine sets in use. Closed exhaust in turbine
28,800		
"	3 hours	D. Without closed exhaust
2/5th power	3 hours	Under conditions C

SHP	Period	Remarks
57,600		
"	3 hours	Under conditions D
3/5ths power	3 hours	Under conditions C
"	3 hours	Under conditions D
4/5ths power	3 hours	Under conditions C
"	3 hours	Under conditions D
Full power	4 hours	Under conditions C
"	4 hours	Under conditions D

An astern trial with half boilers to be carried out as convenient on the termination of any of the above trials.

The ship to be steamed by naval ratings, the workings of the machinery and boilers to be under the supervision of the main machinery contractors.

Arrangements are being made for a Trial Record Party from drawing office staffs of the Dockyards. This record staff will be under the supervision of an officer from the Engineer-in-Chief's department.

9. Report on *Hood*'s Gun Trials.

S V Goodall to Mr Attwood,

I attended these trials on March 26th.

The trials of 5.5" guns were carried out first, four rounds with full charges being fired from each gun. The angles of elevation were :- horizontal, 5° elevation, extreme elevation with flat nosed projectile and at the horizontal with the gun packed back. A rapid series of ten rounds full charges was fired from one 5.5" gun.

So far DNC is concerned, the results are very satisfactory. It was interesting to observe the working of the guns' crews on account of the height of the gun and the impression left upon was, that in a new design, some method must be schemed out whereby such large

angles of elevation can be obtained without the breech being so high above the platform on which the gun's crew works.

Four rounds were fired from each of the 4" QFV guns on HAIII mountings and a rapid series of ten rounds was fired from each gun. So far as DNC is concerned the results were quite satisfactory: there was no indication of lack of stiffness under the gun mounted over the Admiral's after cabin. In some cases the brass case was not discharged from the breech after the gun was fired and the so-called rapid series was for this reason not particularly rapid. The rail at the back of the platform rather interfered with the working of the loading chamber.

Four rounds were fired from each of the 15" guns as follows:-

One round at extreme elevation with flat nosed projectile.
One round at extreme depression packed back.

In 'A' turret the chain between the cordite carrier and the shell carriage broke. The charge was broken up and loose cordite spilt in the hoist. After one of the rounds with the right gun in this turret, a rather severe back flash occurred resulting in the slight scorching of the man working the gun loading cage and the Lieutenant who was standing behind him. Apparently the air blast was being worked by hand and was not turned on sufficiently quick after the breech was opened.

During the firings from 'B' turret I was stationed either in the 15" spotting top or the main director tower on the foremast. At the fore end of the former position the movement caused by the firing of the gun was very marked, but in my opinion, not unduly so considering the overhang and in the latter position the movement was not more than I have experienced in similar positions in other ships, notably, Furious when firing an 18" gun and New Mexico

when firing a 14" salvo.

A warrant officer was present in the director tower who stated that it was his duty to work the director and he appeared quite satisfied that the tower support was sufficiently rigid. In 'B' turret a chain was broken similarly to the occurrence in 'A' turret except that this did not result in the breaking up of the charge.

During the firings from 'X' turret I was in the magazine handling room where nothing unusual occurred. A chain again broke in the hoist. The 3rd round from 'X' turret was fired at extreme elevation and at an angle of training about 25° before the beam on the port side. This resulted in damage to the cabin recently erected in the space formerly occupied by a 5.5" gun.

During the firings from 'Y' turret I was present in the working chamber. Trouble was again experienced with the hoist.

So far as DNC is concerned the results were quite satisfactory. No unusual deflections of the structure were observed.

Owing to the trouble with the hoists, the rapid series that was to be fired from 'B' turret was omitted from the programme.

10. Instructions for Riveting

The following instructions applied to riveting of oil-tight compartments and were attached to shipbuilder's drawings of *Hood*.

All riveting in oil-tight work is to be done with the utmost care. The use of the drift punch is absolutely prohibited. All unfair holes are to be rimered and larger rivets fitted in the rimered holes.

The steel surface must be in absolute contact when no stopwaters are fitted and care must be taken to remove all burrs due to punching, shearing etc, particles of drilled or rimered materials from between the surfaces before the work is screwed up.

Stopwaters must be fitted for three ply and difficult work generally.

Brown paper coated with hard yellow soap, and yarn coated with hard yellow soap, have been found satisfactory. Where injections are necessary, yellow soap with Portland cement, and yellow soap alone, have been found to give good results. Parax composition may also be used for bedding in special cases if approval is previously obtained.

No red lead to be used in contact with oil-tight work.

All holes for rivets which pass through three or more thicknesses of mild steel plating, angles etc are to be drilled through all the thicknesses except one of the outer.

SOURCES AND BIBLIOGRAPHY

Primary Sources

National Maritime Museum
Ships' Covers
HMS *Inflexible* ADM/138/285 and 285
HMS *Australia* ADM/138/324 and 325
HMS *Tiger* ADM/138/420
HMS *Repulse* ADM/138/463 and 464
HMS *Hood* ADM138/449 to 452

University of Glasgow Archives
The extensive archives of John Brown & Co and in particular :
UCS 1/1/1 Board Minutes
UCS 1/1/13 Minutes 1899-1910
UCS 1/5/5 to 19 (the period 1905 to 1920)
UCS 1/10/1 to 3 Shipyard Diary
UCS 1/11/4 to 5 Letter Books August 1910 to December 1910
UCS 1/11/6 to 10 Correspondence with Charles Curtis
UCS 1/13/21 Official letter books
UCS 1/21/19 Cancelled Contracts
UCS 1/52/3 Pay Bill Books
UCS 1/59/1 to 3 Employment returns HMS *Repulse*
UCS 1/74/5 to 7 Tender Books covering period 1905 to 1920

UCS 1/76/2 Contracts Costs Register No2
UCS 1/80/2 Hull Costs Book No 11 and 12
UCS 1/86/20 Comparison of Costs
UCS 1/107/81 Cancelled battlecruiser files

The National Archives of Scotland
The photographic collection of John Brown & Co Ltd.

Books
Brown, David K, *The Grand Fleet, Warship Design and Development 1906–1922* (Chatham Publishing, London, 1999).
Burt, R A, *British Battleships of World War 1* (Arms & Armour Press, London, 1986).
_____, *British Battleships 1919-1939* (Arms & Armour Press, London, 1993).
Gardiner, Robert (ed), *Conway's All the World's Fighting Ships, 1906–1921* (Conway Maritime Press, London, 1985).
Johnston, Ian, *Ships for a Nation, John Brown & Co Clydebank 1847–1971* (Ian Johnston, West Dunbartonshire Libraries and Museums, 2001).
Raven, Alan, and John Roberts, *British Battleships of World War Two* (Arms & Armour Press, London, 1976).
Roberts, John, *Battlecruisers* (Chatham Publishing, London, 1997).

INDEX